Invisible Universe

The Electromagnetic Spectrum from Radio Waves to Gamma Rays

Grades 6–8
(can be adapted for 9 and above)

Skills
Observing • Inferring • Graphing • Analyzing Data • Visualizing
Drawing Conclusions • Explaining • Communicating

Concepts
Astronomy • Energy • Detectors • Emitters • Nature of Waves
Types of Electromagnetic (EM) Energy • The Electromagnetic Spectrum
Gamma-Ray Bursts • Scale of and Objects in the Universe

Themes
Models and Simulations • Systems and Interactions • Patterns of Change
Scale • Diversity and Unity

Mathematics Strands
Number • Measurement • Geometry • Decimal Notation
Powers of Ten • Logic and Language

Nature of Science and Mathematics
Changing Nature of Facts and Theories • Interdisciplinary
Science and Technology • Real-Life Applications

Time
Five 45–60 minute sessions
(Activities 2 and 5 may extend to two class sessions)

by

Stephen Pompea and **Alan Gould**

with **Lincoln Bergman**

LHS GEMS

Great Explorations in Math and Science
Lawrence Hall of Science
University of California at Berkeley

Cover Design
Carol Bevilacqua

Illustrations
Lisa Haderlie Baker
Alan Gould

Photographs
Sam Willard
Alan Gould
Stephen Pompea

Lawrence Hall of Science, University of California,
Berkeley, CA 94720-5200

Director: Elizabeth K. Stage

Publication of *Invisible Universe* was made possible by a grant from the NASA Swift Mission Education and Public Outreach Program, NASA grant #NAG5-9495. The GEMS Program and the Lawrence Hall of Science greatly appreciate this support.

Initial support for the origination and publication of the GEMS series was provided by the A.W. Mellon Foundation and the Carnegie Corporation of New York. Under a grant from the National Science Foundation, GEMS Leader's Workshops have been held across the country. GEMS has also received support from the McDonnell-Douglas Foundation and Employee's Community Fund; Employees Community Fund of Boeing California and the Boeing Corporation; the Hewlett Packard Company; the people at Chevron USA; the William K. Holt Foundation; Join Hands, the Health and Safety Educational Alliance; the Microscopy Society of America (MSA); the Shell Oil Company Foundation; and the Crail-Johnson Foundation. GEMS also gratefully acknowledges the contribution of word processing equipment from Apple Computer, Inc. This support does not imply responsibility for statements or views expressed in publications of the GEMS program. For further information on GEMS leadership opportunities, or to receive a catalog and the *GEMS Network News,* please contact GEMS at the address and phone number below. We also welcome letters to the *GEMS Network News.*

Printed on recycled paper with soy-based inks.

International Standard Book Number: 0-924886-69-2

**Visit GEMS at
www.lhsgems.org**

COMMENTS WELCOME !

Great Explorations in Math and Science (GEMS) is an ongoing curriculum development program. GEMS guides are periodically revised to incorporate teacher comments and new approaches. We welcome your suggestions, criticisms, and helpful hints, and any anecdotes about your experience presenting GEMS activities. Your suggestions will be reviewed each time a GEMS guide is revised. Please send your comments to: GEMS Revisions, c/o Lawrence Hall of Science, University of California, Berkeley, CA 94720-5200. The phone number is (510) 642-7771 and the fax number is (510) 643-0309. You can also reach us by e-mail at gems@uclink.berkeley.edu, or visit our website at www.lhsgems.org

Great Explorations in Math and Science (GEMS) Program

The Lawrence Hall of Science (LHS) is a public science center on the University of California at Berkeley campus. LHS offers a full program of activities for the public, including workshops and classes, exhibits, films, lectures, and special events. LHS is also a center for teacher education and curriculum research and development.

Over the years, LHS staff has developed a multitude of activities, assembly programs, classes, and interactive exhibits. These programs have proven immensely successful at the Hall and should be useful to schools, other science centers, museums, and community groups. A number of these guided-discovery activities have been published under the Great Explorations in Math and Science (GEMS) title, after an extensive refinement and adaptation process that includes classroom testing of trial versions and modifications to ensure the use of easy-to-obtain materials. Carefully written and edited step-by-step instructions and background information allow presentation by teachers without special background in mathematics or science.

Staff

Director: Jacqueline Barber
Associate Director: Kimi Hosoume
Associate Director/Principal Editor: Lincoln Bergman
Mathematics Curriculum Specialist: Jaine Kopp
GEMS Network Director: Carolyn Willard
GEMS Workshop Coordinator: Laura Tucker
Staff Development Specialists: Lynn Barakos, Katharine Barrett, Kevin Beals, Ellen Blinderman, John Erickson, Stan Fukunaga, Karen Ostlund
Distribution Coordinator: Karen Milligan
Workshop Administrator: Terry Cort
Trial Test and Materials Manager: Cheryl Webb
Financial Assistant: Vivian Tong

Distribution Representative: Felicia Roston
Shipping Assistant: Justin Holley
Director of Marketing: Steve Dunphy
Senior Writer: Nicole Parizeau
Editor: Florence Stone
Principal Publications Coordinator: Kay Fairwell
Art Director: Lisa Haderlie Baker
Senior Artists: Carol Bevilacqua, Lisa Klofkorn
Staff Assistants: Haleah Hoshino, Mikalyn Roberts, Thania Sanchez, Stacey Touson

Contributing Authors

Jacqueline Barber
Katharine Barrett
Kevin Beals
Lincoln Bergman
Susan Brady
Beverly Braxton
Kevin Cuff

Linda De Lucchi
Gigi Dornfest
Jean C. Echols
John Erickson
Philip Gonsalves
Jan M. Goodman

Alan Gould
Catherine Halversen
Debra Harper
Kimi Hosoume
Susan Jagoda
Jaine Kopp

Linda Lipner
Larry Malone
Cary I. Sneider
Craig Strang
Herbert Thier
Jennifer Meux White
Carolyn Willard

Reviewers

We would like to thank the following educators who reviewed, tested, or coordinated the reviewing of this series of GEMS guides, including *Algebraic Reasoning for Grades 3–5, Electric Circuits, Invisible Universe,* and *Living with a Star.* Their critical comments and recommendations, based on classroom presentation of these activities nationwide, contributed significantly to this publication. Participation in this review process does not necessarily imply endorsement of the GEMS program or responsibility for statements or views expressed. Classroom testing is a recognized and invaluable hallmark of GEMS curriculum development; feedback is carefully recorded and integrated as appropriate into the publications. **THANK YOU!**

ARIZONA

Liberty School District #25, Buckeye
Wayne Bryan*
Terri Matteson

Arrowhead Elementary School, Phoenix
Noel Fasano
Jorjanne Miller
Kimberly Rimbey*
Delores Salisz
George Sowby
Coreen Weber

Hohokam Middle School, Tucson
Maria Federico-Brummer
Jennine Grogan*

Pistor Middle School, Tucson
Mike Ellis*

ARKANSAS

Carl Stuart Middle School, Conway
Chris Bing
Linda Dow
Gene Hodges
Charlcie Strange*

CALIFORNIA

Albany Middle School, Albany
Kay Sorg*

Rio Del Mar Elementary School, Aptos
Chris Ferrero
Doug Kyle
Tom LaHue*
Debbie Lawheed

Endeavor Elementary, Bakersfield
Matthew Diggle
Jan Karnowski*
Carolyn Reinen
Julie Rosales

Le Conte Elementary, Berkeley
Carole Chin*
Lorna Cross
Jennifer Smallwood

Longfellow Middle School, Berkeley
Karen Bush*

Juan Crespi Junior High School, El Sobrante
Randa Emera*
Juli Goldwyn
Geri Lommen
Julie Skow*

Oak Manor School, Fairfax
Celia Cuomo

Lorin Eden Elementary School, Hayward
Donna Goldenstein*
Elise Tran

M. H. Stanley Intermediate School, Lafayette
Tina Woodworth

Altamont Creek Elementary, Livermore
Pauline Huben*
Janice Louthan

Emma C. Smith Elementary, Livermore
J. Gulbransen

Leo R. Croche Elementary, Livermore
Corinne Agurkis

Mammoth Elementary School, Mammoth Lakes
Sue Barker*
Sandy Bramble
Stacey Posey
Janis Richardson

Cypress Elementary, Newbury Park
Cheryl Bowen
Christina Myren*
Kim Thompson

Bret Harte Middle School, Oakland
Anthony Cody

Roosevelt Middle School, Oakland
Ileana de la Torre
Suzanne Frechette
Elizabeth (Betsy) Rosenberg*

Sobrante Park Elementary, Oakland
Teri Hudson*
Paul McDermott
Raul Nunez
Julie Pokrivnak

Westlake Middle School, Oakland
Hindatu Mohammed*

Los Medanos Elementary, Pittsburg
Tanya Duke*
Syglenda Ford
Karen Staats
Delores Williams

Creekside Middle School, Rohnert Park
Emily Dunnagan
Al Janulaw*
Bonny Stene

Baldwin Elementary, San Jose
Beth Harris
Marietta Harris
Brenda Hough*
Shelley McCracken

Downer Elementary School, San Pablo
Antoineta Franco
Melinda Melaugh
Diana Ortega
Amy Scott
Emily Vogler

Rincon Valley Middle School, Santa Rosa
Jim Bennett
Penny Sirota*
Laurel VarnBuhler

Acacia Elementary, Thousand Oaks
Banny Anderson
Karen Barker
Cathy Bostic
Sharon Sickler

Meadows Elementary, Thousand Oaks
Laura Nedwick

Glen Cove Elementary, Vallejo
Cindy Jones
Diana McKeever
Charles Shannon*

COLORADO

Cory Elementary School, Denver
Debbie Beard
Scott Sala*

FLORIDA

Howard Middle School, Orlando
Hassan Champion
Susan Leeds*
Nicole Ryker

ILLINOIS

Sandwich Middle School, Sandwich
Angela Knierim*
Krista Olson
Kim Paulus
Amy Sigler

OHIO

Cameron Park Elementary, Cincinnati
Cris Cornelssen
Kris Thompson

Lakeside Elementary, Cincinnati
Bob Flinn*
Stacey Owens

Jewish Education Center of Cleveland, Cleveland Heights
Elaine Feigenbaum
Ida Friedman-Kasdan
Eugenia Johnson-Whitt*
Jill Leve
Rabbi Reich

Fairfield North Elementary School, Hamilton
Carol Gregory
Carolyn Kolkmeyer
Sheila Messersmith
Wendy New*
Sheila Webb

Wilmington Middle School, Wilmington
Jeff Bourne
Gary Downing
Sue Hanna
Amy Steinle*
Kathy Vincent

OREGON

Redwood Elementary School, Grants Pass
Shelly Brandes
Lorelei Dean
Renee Grant*
Marleen Knight

Kennedy Elementary, Medford
Carol Fitspatrick
Teena Staller*

Lone Pine Elementary, Medford
Madolyn Malloy

Oak Grove Elementary, Medford
Cheryl Lemke

Portland Lutheran School, Portland
Karin Maier*
Ruth Mannion
Desi Pritchard
Tom Zuch

PENNSYLVANIA

Crossroads Middle School, Lewisberry
Carol Brame
Hannah Leigey*

Fairview Elementary School, New Cumberland
Beth Erikson
Julie Estep
Louise Shuey
Sue White

SOUTH CAROLINA

McCormick Elementary School, Mullins
Barbara Baker
Debbie Beeson
Sarah Dew
Patricia Grant
Brenda Ladson
Fannie Mason*

College Park Middle School, Summerville
Dottie Adams
Marsha Lindsay*

Sangaree Intermediate School, Summerville
Deanna Hefner
Sandy Wiedmeyer*

TENNESSEE

Bartlett Elementary School, Bartlett
Penny Blair
Jenny Carter
Joyce Cornett
Jill Crumpton*
Anne Faulks*
LaJuana Heaston
Lee Loft
Portia Tate
Jenny Underwood

TEXAS

Bammel Elementary, Houston
Anna Dugger
Tracey Harros*
Staci Horan
Cindy Lane

Clear Creek ISD, Seabrook
Christine Casaburri
Susan Lallo
Ann Martinez
Katherine Mays
Sandy Peck*
Sally Wall

WASHINGTON

Covington Middle School, Vancouver
Laurie Cripe*
Bryce Hampton
Marie Morasch
Jackie Serniotti

*Trial Test Coordinators

Acknowledgments

This guide—like a number of others in the GEMS series—owes its very existence to the high level of educational awareness of the National Aeronautics and Space Administration (NASA). NASA recognizes the importance of public education and outreach to students of all ages, and each NASA mission has an Education and Public Outreach component. One of the educational efforts of the exciting NASA Swift Mission, described in this guide and scheduled for launch in 2003, is this *Invisible Universe* teacher's guide. We should also point out that the incredible collections of space images available from NASA and its many branches and projects—many of them available electronically—were obviously of enormous benefit in putting this unit together!

The authors very gratefully acknowledge the direct involvement in this guide's development of Dr. Lynn Cominsky and Dr. Laura Whitlock, in connection with the educational efforts of the NASA Swift Mission. They provided extremely helpful input during all stages of trial testing, as well as expert scientific review. In the final scientific review of this unit we are especially appreciative of the incisive and detailed comments of Tom Arnold, Pennsylvania State University master teacher on the Swift Education Committee (SwEC), Tim Graves, instructional technology consultant in the Education and Public Outreach Group at Sonoma State University, Dr. Brad Schaefer, astrophysicist at the University of Texas at Austin, and Lynn Cominsky. The wonderful story about a swift and an astronomer (pages 106–7) was written in Italian by Monica Sperandio, an astronomer working with the Italian branch of the Swift mission, translated by Giuliana Giobbi, and edited for this guide by Lincoln Bergman.

In addition to the authors, a very important contribution to this guide was made by Kevin Beals and David Glaser, Lawrence Hall of Science educators and GEMS curriculum developers, who originated and pilot tested Activity 2, "Invisible Light Sources and Detectors." Thanks to Anthony Cody, 6th grade teacher at Bret Harte Middle School in Oakland, for sharing his students with us in the pilot testing. Thanks as well to Carolyn Willard of GEMS for her ever-cogent classroom wisdom and practical suggestions and to Florence Stone, GEMS Editor, for researching resources and literature connections.

As always, we are extremely appreciative of the dedicated efforts of teachers all across the country who tested this unit in their classrooms and provided detailed and very helpful feedback. They are listed in the front of the guide. Last, but far from least, this book is dedicated to their inquiring students and all students everywhere. As human exploration of space continues—as scientific understanding of all the regions of the electromagnetic spectrum increases—it is the students of today who will contribute to new discoveries that we cannot yet even envision!

Contents

Swift is Launched!

On November 20, 2004 the NASA Swift satellite was successfully launched into orbit, with three different telescopes designed to learn more about gamma ray bursts. The NASA Swift mission supported the development of this GEMS teacher's guide as part of its education and public outreach programs. As suggested in the guide, you and your students may want to track the ongoing observations and findings of the Swift mission. For more on Swift, see http://swift.sonoma.edu/

Crab Nebula as seen in visible light:

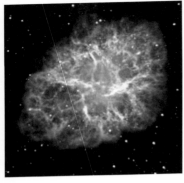

Crab Nebula as seen using radio telescope:

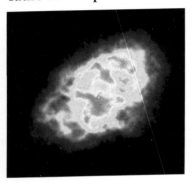

Crab Nebula as seen in ultraviolet light:

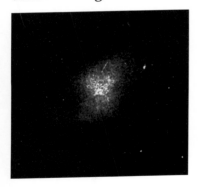

Crab Nebula as seen using an X-ray telescope:

Introduction

This guide introduces your students to the mystery of gamma-ray bursts as a gateway and motivation for gaining fundamental understandings of waves and the different wavelengths of the electromagnetic spectrum. At the same time, students gain current insight into cutting-edge issues in modern astronomy and space science.

In this unit, students consider how our everyday world and the cosmos look when they are "observed" in other wavelengths, as if we had infrared, radio, or X-ray sensitive eyes. What would the gamma-ray Universe look like? Can exploring in other wavelengths help us solve mysteries, like the source or sources of gamma-ray bursts?

Like a horse wearing blinders, humans see only a thin, restricted portion of the electromagnetic spectrum. Beyond our view is a whole **"invisible Universe,"** filled with rays of electromagnetic energy at wavelengths of light we cannot see. Modern astronomers, eagerly seeking views of this invisible Universe, are rapidly constructing special detectors for these invisible rays, and then launching these detectors into space, above Earth's absorbing atmosphere. From this vantagepoint the Universe looks completely different. It is not only different from our eye- and Earth-based view, but each wavelength—from radio waves to gamma rays—gives us further information about what is out there, and how it may have originated.

One of the biggest mysteries in space observations of the last 30 years is gamma-ray bursts. These incredibly powerful bursts of radiation from space were first detected by military satellites looking for nuclear explosions violating the Nuclear Test Ban Treaty. After a fraction of a second or at most a few hundred seconds, the source of the gamma-ray burst disappears and is not seen again. Later, in another part of the sky, another burst appears. Flashes are detected about once a day. The energy of these bursts is almost too fantastic to believe—over a hundred billion times the energy being released by our Sun. What is happening in the Universe that could generate such an impressive amount of energy? Can it be explained by the creation of black holes or by some other unusual cosmological phenomena? With the launch of X-ray and gamma-ray observatories, we are on the verge of understanding more about gamma-ray bursts. At this point, their origin remains a mystery.

With the mystery of the gamma-ray bursts as a motivational theme of the unit, it becomes necessary for students to gain the prerequisite knowledge and ideas that can lead to understanding the mystery, even though it has not yet been solved. These precursor concepts come into play as students learn about: waves and wave motion (Activity 1); invisible waves (Activity 2); the entire electromagnetic spectrum (Activity 3); distances to celestial objects (Activity 4); and then gain a sense of the huge amounts of energy that can be released in cosmic events and learn how astronomers plan to further investigate the mystery of gamma-ray bursts (Activity 5).

We strongly recommend that you read through the entire guide to familiarize yourself with the activities and their progression before presenting the unit to students. You may also want to familiarize yourself with the "Background for the Teacher" section, with a glossary, concise information on the electromagnetic spectrum, and other topics.

Summary of the Activities

Activity 1: Comparing Wave Makers

A series of news flashes sets the stage for the unit by introducing the mystery of gamma-ray bursts. To work toward understanding gamma rays as very high energy waves, students first investigate properties of simple waves produced in different media. Waves on a spring show basic properties such as wavelength and frequency. Students compare properties in waves that they generate with a variety of wave makers, including two kinds of springs, a rope, a coiled telephone cord, and a water "ripple tank." They record the maximum number of wavelengths each wave maker can sustain and how well waves of various frequencies can be generated.

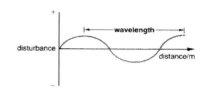

Activity 2: Invisible Light Sources and Detectors

Students work at different learning stations to explore different kinds of light energy and how they can be detected, emitted, and absorbed. Stations include radio (AM and FM), ultraviolet, infrared (lamp and remote control device) and visible light. They then "reflect" on their experiences and are introduced to the idea that there are invisible light energies all around us, and all are part of the electromagnetic spectrum.

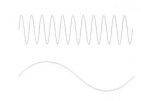

Activity 3: Putting the Electromagnetic Spectrum Together

In this activity, students have an opportunity to sort cards that contain information about the main regions of the electromagnetic spectrum. They are first encouraged to sort the cards in any way they choose, then are introduced to the way scientists generally sequence them. In the process students gain information about each of the regions, and learn how the different regions can be sequenced by their wavelengths and energies.

Activity 4: Tour of the Invisible Universe

This presentation is intended to help students improve their understanding of objects in the Universe, including those connected with gamma-ray bursts. Students can be confused about the terms Solar System, Milky Way Galaxy, and Universe. In this tour, students categorize objects into (1) those in the Solar System, (2) those in the Milky Way *outside* the Solar System, and (3) those beyond the Milky Way. They gain insight into the important role detection in different electromagnetic wavelengths plays in modern astronomy.

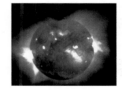

Activity 5: The Most Powerful Explosions in the Universe!

Students return to the gamma-ray burst mystery that opened the unit. Since it is so difficult for anyone to grasp the amount of energy unleashed every day in space, students climb a mental ladder of "energetic events," starting with a car crash, through dynamite explosions, earthquakes, H-bombs, the Sun, and finally to truly awesome gamma-ray bursts. Students make a series of graphs to represent the level of energy of these events. Mathematically, this graphing activity can also serve as a conceptual prelude to student understanding of a logarithmic (or exponential) scale. A student reading provides more background on gamma-ray bursts. Students design an "electromagnificent" poster and learn about the NASA Swift Mission to investigate gamma-ray bursts.

Using the Invisible to Make the Universe Visible

There are two overarching themes in this unit. One focuses on the electromagnetic spectrum and its properties, with emphasis on regions other than visible light. The other introduces modern approaches and findings in astronomy/space science that derive from instruments that detect non-visible regions of the spectrum, including gamma rays.

The title of the guide, while intriguing, could be misleading if taken literally. The Universe, of course, is not invisible! True, there are vast areas we cannot actually see with our eyes due to distance and many other factors. Modern telescopes can extend our vision—in the wavelengths of visible light energy—much farther than could have been imagined for most of human history. The ability to launch visible light telescopes into space, like the Hubble telescope, has further extended and clarified our vision by leapfrogging above the Earth's atmosphere. Yet, as your students learn in this unit, the range of visible light is only a tiny sliver of the electromagnetic spectrum.

The ability to detect and generate images from other wavelengths— invisible wavelengths—on the spectrum has greatly extended our knowledge of the Universe, its workings, changes, and origins. In this sense, this unit is actually about using invisible rays of energy to make the Universe more "visible!" From radio waves to gamma rays, humans have found ways to utilize all the other regions of the electromagnetic spectrum to find out more about the Universe than visible light alone can tell us. The new and fascinating insights to be glimpsed and recorded—the many important discoveries to be made—have only just begun!

Learning Goals, Standards, and Assessment

Major learning goals for this unit are articulated in the "Assessment Suggestions" section and summarized in overviews to each main activity. This unit includes a number of related learning goals that build to an increased understanding of the electromagnetic spectrum, its regions, and their distinguishing characteristics. This is an important content area in the physical sciences and has major impact in many aspects of our lives. This learning connects directly to national science education standards, as well as to state and district guidelines. Several activities also have strong mathematics content.

While full conceptual understanding of the electromagnetic spectrum is generally seen as within the curricular purview of high school (and above!), many building blocks toward that understanding are appropriate for middle school students and extremely beneficial for their eventual grasp of more advanced science, as well as for their understanding of the role science plays in our daily lives, and the decisions they as citizens will contribute to making about space exploration and the uses of technology. In addition, the unit contributes to student understanding of the nature of science as an ever-questioning process. They learn how gamma-ray bursts were first detected and that their origin is still a mystery. Hopefully, they will track the progress of the Swift satellite, and gain an increased interest in the fascinating research planned by future NASA missions and by the international space science community.

National Science Education Content Standards

• Grades 5–8 Physical Science—Transfer of Energy: The Sun is a major source of energy for changes on the Earth's surface. The Sun loses energy by emitting light. A tiny fraction of that light reaches the Earth, transferring energy from the Sun to the Earth. The Sun's energy arrives as light with a range of wavelengths, consisting of visible light, infrared, and ultraviolet radiation.

• Grades 9–12 Physical Science: Energy can be transferred by collisions in chemical and nuclear reactions, by light waves and other radiations, and in many other ways…All energy can be considered to be either kinetic energy, which is the energy of motion; potential energy, which depends on relative position; or energy contained by a field, such as electromagnetic waves…Waves, including sound and seismic waves, waves on water, and light waves, have energy and can transfer energy when they interact with matter…Electromagnetic waves include radio waves (the longest wavelength), microwaves, infrared radiation (radiant heat), visible light, ultraviolet radiation, X-rays, and gamma rays. The energy of electromagnetic waves is carried in packets whose magnitude is inversely proportional to the wavelength.

National Mathematics Content Standards

• Grades 6–8, 9–12—Numbers and Operations: Understand numbers, ways of representing numbers, relationships among numbers, and number systems. Develop an understanding of large numbers and recognize and appropriately use exponential, scientific, and calculator notation.

• Grades 6–8, 9–12—Measurement: Understand measurable attributes of objects and the units, systems, and processes of measurement. Understand relationships among units and convert from one unit to another within the same system. Make decisions about units and scales that are appropriate for problem situations involving measurement.

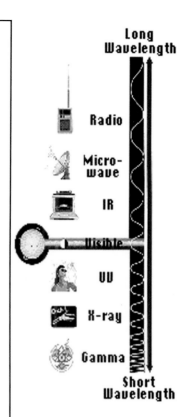

Long Wavelength

Radio

Micro-wave

IR

Visible

UV

X-ray

Gamma

Short Wavelength

GAMMA-RAY BURSTS

Activity 1: Comparing Wave Makers

Overview

Through a short dramatic reading that opens the unit, students are introduced to the mystery of gamma-ray bursts. The teacher explains that to gain a deeper understanding of how this mystery might be solved, students need to understand more about waves. In this first activity, following a teacher demonstration with student volunteers, groups of students visit classroom stations to make observations of waves, including waves on a spring and waves in water. Through their observations, students learn about wavelength, frequency, and other important wave attributes. This activity sets the stage conceptually for deeper understanding of the electromagnetic spectrum in subsequent class sessions.

This activity helps give students a concrete visualization of the wave model of electromagnetic energy. This model suggests that energy—whether it be visible light, radio signals, or gamma rays—travels and spreads out as it goes, in wave-like patterns. A wavelength is the distance between two peaks of a wave. Our eyes can perceive only a small part of the entire electromagnetic spectrum—between certain specific wavelengths. Gaining a basic understanding of wave motion is an important element of physics, and is a very helpful way for people to visualize and gain insight into the invisible energies that race throughout our world and the Universe.

Special Note: Waves provide a particularly excellent model to describe the parts, or regions, of the electromagnetic spectrum where energies are lower, such as radio waves or even visible light waves. When the energy gets higher, such as for X-rays and gamma rays, it is often more useful to describe that part of the spectrum with a particle or photon (particle of light) model. In that case each particle of light has an energy associated with it. To encompass both aspects, electromagnetic energy can be described as both waves and particles. Historically, this became known as the "wave-particle" duality. Which model is used at any given time can differ, depending on what phenomena are being observed, and on what types of detectors are used. For the purposes of initial understanding, the wave model can provide a useful way for students to approach learning about the electromagnetic spectrum.

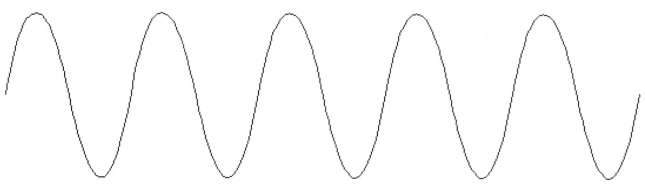

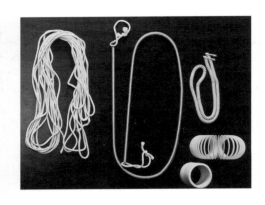

Optional: Commercial wave
machine (from science
supply company)

Diagram of one possible classroom arrangement

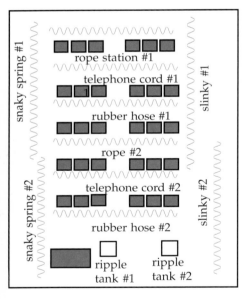

In most situations, a rope
or a hose are best used on
the floor, keeping the waves
on the floor going with a
horizontal motion. Springs
can sustain vertical or
horizontal waves.

What You Need

For the class:

❑ 6 copies of the News Flashes (master on page 24)
❑ 2 overhead projectors
❑ 2 slinkies
❑ 2 metal "snaky" springs—about 5-8 meters (15–25') long when
    stretched out (available from science supply companies)
❑ 2 ropes—thick, heavy, about 5 meters (15') long
❑ 2 coiled telephone wires—about 5 meters (15') long
❑ 2 flexible rubber or plastic hoses—about 5–8 meters (15–25') long
❑ 1 pitcher for water
❑ 2 Ripple Tanks—*For each ripple tank you need:*
  __ 1 flat bottomed clear plastic tray 16 qt. storage box -or- picture
      frame 10" x 10" x 2" or more
  __ 2 pencils or pencil-sized dowels
  __ 1 eye dropper
  __ 2 clear rulers
❑ 1 compass, ideally a transparent one for use on an overhead
❑ 1 inexpensive magnet

For each group of 3 students

❑ 1 meter stick or tape measure

For each student

❑ 1 Handout, *Comparing Wave Makers* (master on page 23)

Getting Ready

1. Obtain all the materials in the list above.

2. Connect two of the slinkies together to make a double
length slinky by overlapping about 6–10 cm of the ends of
each and securing the ends together with duct tape.

3. Set up pairs of stations around the room for the
wave makers—two each of the following:

  • snaky spring   • slinky   • ripple tank
  • rope   • telephone cord   • rubber hose

*Note: The number of stations you will need to set up depends on the size of
your class. Each group of three students needs to be able to visit one of each type
of station (rope, slinky, spring, etc.) So, for example, five pairs of stations (ten
stations in all) would be enough for a class of 30 students. In that case, you'd
choose five of the six suggested wave makers and set up two stations for each of
the five. **Ideally, try to find a larger space (multipurpose room) or do the
activity outdoors.** You may be able to fit it all in your classroom if you arrange
all the desks/tables to form corridors long enough to stretch out the wavemakers.
Chairs can be stacked on top of the tables to open more floor area. The diagram on
this page shows one sample arrangement for a classroom with individual desks,
but, if possible, a larger space is preferable.*

4. Put handles on the snaky springs to make them easier to hold. To do this, take two pieces of clothesline or rope, each about 50 cm(20 inches) long, and tie them on the ends of the spring for handles.

5. The set-up for each ripple tank is a clear glass or plastic pan on an overhead projector. Put water in the pan about 1–3 cm deep.

6. Photocopy a *Comparing Wave Makers* worksheet (master on page 23) for each student (or make a transparency of it and have students design their own worksheets on blank paper). Make six copies of the "Mystery of the Gamma-Ray Bursts" *News Flashes sheet* (page 24) for students to read out loud.

You can customize the worksheet, deleting or adding column headings, depending on which stations you set up.

The Mystery of the Gamma-Ray Bursts

1. Ask six students to read aloud the news flashes on page 24. Urge them to read dramatically, clearly, and not too fast. Following the reading, ask students if they have questions and briefly discuss. Say scientists still have many questions they are investigating. Explain that gamma rays are invisible rays or waves of electromagnetic energy.

2. Ask students what the mystery described by the news flashes is and accept several responses. As needed, emphasize that one of the biggest mysteries is what could cause gamma-ray bursts. Tell them that astronomers are now detecting these enormously powerful bursts of energy about once a day! What could be happening in the Universe to generate such huge amounts of energy? That's a big mystery and it's still unsolved.

3. Explain that, as in any other mystery, scientists, like detectives, are curious about what's happening, ask questions to find out more, and gather and analyze all the evidence they can find. Say that to find out more about the gamma-ray burst mystery, they will investigate waves of invisible energy, many of which we make use of every day.

4. Then ask yourself and the class— "What does it really mean to talk about **'waves** of invisible energy?'" Tell students that one logical place to start finding out what this means and to learn more about the gamma-ray burst mystery is to investigate **waves** themselves, how they can be made, and how they behave in different materials.

Demonstrating Waves

1. Emphasize to students that a wave model is one way that scientists visualize the movement of energy.

2. Lay the spring (you can't do this with a rope or hose) in a straight line on the floor and hold one side of the spring. Ask a student volunteer to hold the other end.

3. Start by stretching the spring (but not overstretching it). Grab a piece of the spring, pull it up or down, then release it, sending a pulse down the spring. Ask, **"What happens when the wave reaches the end of the spring?"** [At the end it will "reflect" and bounce back.]

A standing wave or "standing wave pattern" occurs when a vibrational pattern set in motion in an object reflects back so the crest of each returning wave meets the crest of each incoming wave at the same place at the same time, making it appear as if there are places that are standing still. This appearance of standing still is what gives them their name. Interaction between the wave that begins and the one that returns is called interference, but in the special case of a standing wave, the two waves exactly align. Standing waves occur at the natural frequencies of an object (a guitar string, for example) and these frequencies are called harmonic frequencies.

Standing Waves Demonstration

1. Demonstrate standing waves, where certain parts of the spring appear motionless and others are moving up and down (or right and left) very fast. (This is fairly easy to do just by moving one end of the spring up and down at a constant rate. The rate determines how many "standing waves" you can generate.)

2. Explain that these standing waves are similar to what happens to strings on musical instruments when they vibrate or to resonances of sound in organ pipes.

3. Ask for another student volunteer to come up and hold your end of the spring. Then ask the volunteer at the other end of the spring to try to make standing waves with one wave cycle, then two—how many can fit on the spring? (The speed that arms can move are the limiting factor, rather than the properties of the spring.)

Defining Wavelength, Frequency, and Amplitude

1. Tell the class that some special terms are used to describe wave patterns. Explain the following definitions to them.

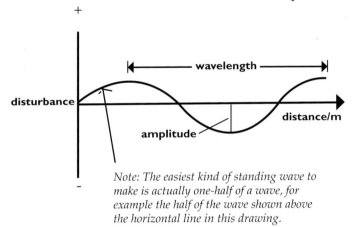

Note: The easiest kind of standing wave to make is actually one-half of a wave, for example the half of the wave shown above the horizontal line in this drawing.

- *Wavelength*—the distance between successive peaks of waves.

- *Frequency*—how often a wave goes by a given point, measured in waves per second or cycles per second. One way to measure frequency is to count how many tops of waves go by a given point in one second. The answer will be in cycles per second.

- *Amplitude*—how far the highest part of the wave is above the middle position.

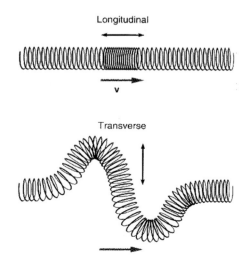

Optional: Explain the difference between two types of waves:

◊ *In a longitudinal wave, the disturbance is in the same direction as the motion of the wave.*

◊ *A transverse wave is set in motion by a disturbance or deflection at right angles to the direction in which the wave is moving.*

2. Ask the students, **"Is there any relationship between wavelength and frequency on this spring?"** Encourage student volunteers to determine the answer by observation and experiment until they see that shaking the end at higher frequencies leads to shorter wavelengths.

3. Give student volunteers an opportunity to create waves of different types and sizes. Then ask the class: **"Is the amplitude (height) of a wave related to wavelength or frequency?"** Encourage student volunteers to determine the answer to this by observation They should discover that amplitude is **not** related to frequency. You can have a large or a small amplitude for any given wavelength or frequency.

4. Ask, **"Which takes more energy to produce: high frequency, shorter wavelength waves *OR* low frequency, longer wavelength waves?"** Have student volunteers determine the answer (or confirm what they already know) through experience—by making waves. Have volunteers return to their seats.

Other Kinds of Waves

1. Ask the class, **"In what other materials can you produce waves?"** [Air (sound waves), water (ocean waves), even at football games (people "waves" made by crowds at sports events).]

2. Point out that waves can be viewed as a flow of information rather than of material or mass. Using the football crowd wave as an example, ask students: **"The wave looks like it's moving sideways, but are people actually moving in the direction that the wave travels?"** [No. The movement of the wave goes around the arena but the people stay in their seats.]

3. Point out that, in a similar way, waves in the open ocean do not really move large amounts of *water* forward in the direction of the wave. A cork on the water goes up and down as the wave goes by but does not really move forward with the wave. The disturbance (the wave) moves forward but the ocean does not. Similarly, the disturbance on the spring moves forward, but the entire spring does not. (These are both examples of a transverse wave.)

Demonstrate the Ripple Tank

1. Tell the class they will soon get a chance to make some waves and experience wave motion for themselves at different stations. Divide the class into groups and explain that they should record data on their *Comparing Wave makers* worksheets. Mention that the springs, rope, and phone cords all behave in a similar way.

2. Before they start, since it is new to the students, demonstrate how to operate the ripple tank as follows:

    a. Put a clear plastic or glass tray filled to a shallow level with water on an overhead projector.

For more advanced classes: Sound is a compression *wave, also called a* longitudinal *wave. Put very simply, a compression wave is like a long line of cars that are very close together but hardly moving. If the car in front of you gets very far ahead, you try to speed up to get closer. The people in that car behind you then speed up to close the gap you created. For sound waves in air, the compression waves are formed from molecules rather than cars. Compression waves can be modeled on the spring by pinching a section of the spring together and letting go.*

b. Pour 1/4 to 1/2 inch of water and add more if it helps. Focus the overhead projector by putting a pencil about an inch above the water and focusing on that point.

c. Explain that there are more ways to create waves with the ripple tank than with the other materials. Demonstrate one or more of these:

> 1) Circular waves can be generated by slowly dropping water drops using a medicine dropper.

> 2) Tap the pencil point vertically into the water to generate waves. You can try the eraser end as well.

> 3) Float a pencil at one end of the tray and tap the tray with another pencil.

> 4) Use a ruler to generate waves. Place it on its long edge at one end of the tray, keeping it vertical in the tray and rock it gently back and forth to create waves.

One GEMS teacher suggested that a transparency of a centimeter graph under the tank would be helpful to students. She added that adding food coloring can make the waves more visible.

3. For the ripple tank, you could ask these additional questions:

"What happens when a wave hits curved barriers?"
"What happens to waves when they go through a gap?"

Ripple tank waves going through different width gaps.

Wave Makers/Students Making Waves

1. Tell students to circulate to the different wave stations, reminding them to fill out their observation sheets. With younger classes, you may want to go over the data sheet with the class first.

2. Circulate around the room to respond to questions that may arise, help with procedures, and keep the student groups moving through the stations.

Reporting Wave Findings

1. Have groups report their findings. Each group can report on a different wave maker and invite other groups to comment, add, or give differing views. **Responses to the questions and related information appears in the box on top of page 22.**

Note: In reporting wave behavior, it is very tempting to say that a high frequency wave is a "fast" wave and that a low frequency wave is a "slow" wave, because to make a high frequency wave you have to shake your hand very fast, and for a low frequency wave, your hand moves slowly. We strongly advise, however, that you discourage this usage, because the actual speed of the wave moving through space is quite different from the frequency, which is the rate of oscillation of a given point on the wave. A much better use of terminology would be high energy waves (for high frequency that requires faster hand movement) and low energy waves (for lower frequency requiring slower hand movement). This terminology is relatively intuitive since it certainly feels like it takes more energy to make the higher energy waves.

2. Review the basics of waves by asking for a volunteer to draw a wave and label the parts. If needed, assist them to put in labels for wavelength, amplitude, and frequency.

3. Remind students that frequency is a measure of how many waves go by per second. That is the same as how many crests of waves go by per second.

Waves Made of Invisible Forces

1. Tell the class that light waves have a frequency of about a hundred million million (10^{14}) times per second! Ask, **"Does anyone know how fast light waves travel?"** [300,000 km/sec or 186,000 mi/sec.]

2. Explain that light is not made of ordinary material, like the springs, rope, or water are. Ask, **"What do you think light waves are made of?"** [Take several responses] Explain that light waves are made of electric and magnetic fields, that light is made of waves of invisible force. Ask, **"Can you think of any other invisible forces?"** [Gravity]

Optional:
*Ask, **"How long would it take a light beam to go from the Earth to the Moon—a distance of 384,000 kilometers, or 238,000 miles?"*** *[1.3 seconds] This is technically an algebra question, especially if you give the class the distance (d), velocity (v), time (t) function from physics:*

distance = velocity x time
or d = vt
Solving for time gives us
t = d/v

3. Demonstrate the "action-at-a-distance" of a magnetic force by moving a magnet close enough to a compass so it deflects the compass needle. (Ideally use a transparent compass on the overhead so the whole class can see at once.) Move the magnet back and forth to make the needle oscillate. Explain that when the magnet moves, the **invisible** field in the space around the magnet also moves, creating a magnetic wave.

Note: If you have the time and equipment, you could have groups of students use magnets and/or compasses to experience the invisible magnetic force in one of the ways shown in the diagrams on this page.

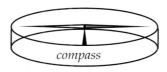 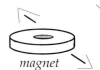

Magnet and compass. *Move the magnet to deflect the compass needle.*

4. Explain that since light waves are made of a combination of electric and magnetic fields, they are called **electromagnetic waves.** Scientists have described and classified the different regions of electromagnetic energy, and the class will explore this idea further in the next class sessions.

> *Note: In everyday speech, we often say "light" when we mean only visible light, like **some** of the light from the Sun or from a light bulb. Scientists, however, often use the word to mean **all** electromagnetic energy, from radio waves to gamma rays.*

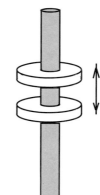

Floating magnets
Another fun way to illustrate the invisible magnetic force is to slide two inexpensive ring-shaped magnets onto a pencil or dowel, and make the upper magnet float on top of the lower one by proper orientation of their north-south poles. Shaking the pencil causes the upper magnet to bob up and down.

5. Return briefly to the mystery of the gamma-ray bursts and explain that gamma rays are electromagnetic waves of *extremely* high frequencies and *very* short wavelengths, much shorter than the width of an atom. The wave cycles of gamma rays are so short that about 10 billion of them would fit across a person's fingernail!

Note: In theory, the speed of a wave in a given material is constant (see "Going Further" discussion below). The emphasis in this activity is on helping students discover the inverse relationship between wavelength and frequency.

Responses to questions on the *Comparing Wave Makers* worksheet:

1. Does increasing the height (amplitude) of a wave seem to affect its speed? [**No.** In theory, the speed with which a wave travels lengthwise does not depend at all on the wave's amplitude.]

2. Does changing the wave's frequency seem to affect the speed of a wave? [**No.** In theory, the speed with which a wave travels lengthwise does not depend at all on the wave's frequency.]

3. Relationship of wavelength with frequency: As the wave's frequency increases, the wavelength: **Decreases**

(See the "Going Further" activity below to further explore the inverse relationship between wavelength and frequency.)

4. Is the relationship between wavelength and frequency (Question 3) the same for all the wave makers?   **Yes**

5. Shaking the end of the wave maker with greater amplitude increases the frequency of the wave.   **False**

Students often try to shake the wave maker harder (higher amplitude) in order get "more waves" (higher frequency)—this seems to be an intuitive strategy. In reality, the only way to get more waves with shorter wavelength (high frequency) is to shake the end of the wave maker more quickly, ***not*** with greater amplitude.

Going Further

To better define the relationship between wavelength and frequency mathematically, have students measure and record wavelengths and frequencies, then graph wavelength versus frequency. This is a standard science/physics exercise or lab. The relationship is an inverse one, governed by the equation:

$$S = \lambda \times f$$

where S = speed (a constant)
        λ = wavelength (is the Greek letter lambda)
        f = frequency (in waves/second)

> *Note:* The Greek letter nu (ν) has classically been used for frequency, but f is more generally used today.

The fact that S is a constant in the equation is an elegant mathematical way to view the answers to questions 1 and 2 on the *Comparing Wave Makers* worksheet.

A good reference about the Greek alphabet on the Web is:
http://www.mathacademy.com/pr/prime/articles/greek/index.asp

Comparing Wave Makers

Name _____

Date _____

	Snaky spring	Slinky	Hose	Rope	Phone Cord	Ripple Tank	
Reflection of single wave pulse observed? (Y = yes; N = no)							
Maximum number of waves achieved?							
Length of shortest wave achieved? (in cm)							
How hard is it to make waves? (On scale of 1–5: with 1=easiest; 5=hardest)							

Questions:

1. The *speed* of a wave is how fast it seems to move lengthwise down the wave maker.
   Does increasing the height (amplitude) of a wave seem to affect its speed?

   Yes No (circle one)

2. The *frequency* of the wave is how quickly you shake the wave maker (number of "shakes" per second). Does changing the wave's frequency seem to affect the speed of a wave?

   Yes No (circle one)

3. Investigating the relationship of wavelength with frequency:
   As the wave's frequency increases, the wavelength

   Increases   Decreases   (circle one)

4. Is the relationship between wavelength and frequency that you determined in Question #3 the same for all the wave makers?

   Yes No (circle one)

5. Shaking the end of the wave maker with greater amplitude increases the frequency of the wave.

   True   False   (circle one)

Analysis and Conclusions (please use other side of sheet as well):

Mystery of the Gamma-Ray Bursts
News Flashes

(read these like a newscaster)

1   **News Flash !** July 1963—President John F. Kennedy, speaking at the White House today, said: "Negotiations were concluded in Moscow on a treaty to ban all nuclear tests in the atmosphere, in outer space, and under water." The President added, "according to the ancient Chinese proverb, 'A journey of a thousand miles must begin with a single step.' Let us, if we can, step back from the shadows of war and seek out the way of peace. And if that journey is a thousand miles, or even more, let history record that we, in this land, at this time, took the first step. Thank you and good night."

2   **News Flash !** October 1963—The U.S. Air Force launched the first in a series of satellites to detect any violations of the Nuclear Test Ban Treaty. The goal is to monitor the Earth, the atmosphere, and even the far side of the Moon to make sure the treaty is being followed. The satellites carry X-ray, gamma-ray, and neutron detectors, since these are produced in nuclear explosions.

3   **News Flash !** From October 1963 on—Good news! No violations of the treaty have been reported up to now. Not one nuclear explosion has been detected on or near the Earth so far!

4   **News Flash !** July 1969—The gamma ray detectors on the satellites show a huge event, a gigantic explosion—not on Earth—not from the Sun—we don't know where this explosion is coming from. It is a mystery of the Universe!

5   **News Flash !** 1973—It is confirmed. At least 16 gigantic gamma-ray bursts have been detected between July 1969 and July 1972. Scientists are rushing to learn more about these newly-discovered bursts sending out invisible rays from space!

6   **News Flash !** *(say today's date)*—Gamma-ray bursts continue and the mystery persists even to this day. Astronomers and other scientists still don't know what is causing them, although they have some theories. There's a mission called the Swift Mission that was launched by NASA in 2004 that hopes to help resolve the mystery.

Activity 2: Invisible Light Sources and Detectors

Overview

X-rays and gamma rays are not and cannot be included as part of this classroom activity because they are dangerous and appropriate sources are difficult to obtain. The X-ray film image does provide a real-life connection to this invisible region on the spectrum. Without understating the serious dangers, it is also important to understand that NOT all instances of radiation are extremely dangerous. Low levels exist all around us as background radiation—from the potassium-40 in our bones and teeth, to uranium chain elements in many types of rock (especially granites), to radon in the atmosphere. There are a range of radioactive materials, and varying levels and amounts of radiation. In some cases, such as X-rays or for cancer therapy, careful use can have real benefits. Controversial social issues involving radiation need to be examined and weighed scientifically, on a case-by-case basis.

We are surrounded by invisible electromagnetic radiation every day. In this activity, students encounter some of those forms of electromagnetic, or light energy.

Students circulate to classroom stations that have different sources of light—most not visible to the human eye. At each station are a variety of objects. After the class discusses which objects are **"detectors"** (they can detect a particular range of visible or invisible light), student groups are challenged to find out which are **"transmitters"** (they allow the invisible light/energy to pass through), and which serve as **"shields"** and are able to block the light. They experiment to see if they can find inventive ways to block the invisible energies. Encouraging students to make predictions is an important aspect of this activity. They should write down their predictions for each station before they experiment with any item.

With the exception of X-rays and gamma rays, (microwave is optional) each station represents a region of the electromagnetic spectrum, as follows:
1. Visible
2. Infrared (lamp)
3. Infrared (VCR/TV remote control unit)
4. Radio (FM)
5. Radio (AM)
6. Ultraviolet (black light bulb)

The main goals of this activity are to give students firsthand experience with invisible electromagnetic energy, and to have them discuss and "reflect" upon it. It's ideal for discussion to follow immediately, but given time constraints, it may carry over to another class session. At the end of the activity, students are introduced to the electromagnetic spectrum, which they learn more about in Activity 3.

What You Need

For the class:

❑ 1 overhead transparency of *Invisible Light Sources, Detectors, and Shields* student sheet
❑ 1 X-ray film image: dental or hospital X-ray transparency
❑ 6–12 Station Number Signs (master on page 38—the quantity will depend on the number of stations you set up).
❑ 6–12 sets of shields/transmitters—one for each station in a manila folder or envelope. Each set has the following materials:

This activity requires substantial preparation, but teachers who tested the unit said it was well worth it—both from the standpoint of strengthening student conceptual understanding and because of its very high level of student interest and motivation.

Optional: *Other useful objects could include anti-static plastic bag, glass microscope slides, eyeglass lenses of all types, or a Pyrex glass pan or beaker filled with water. You could also use a cell phone or pager (for extra microwave station or demonstration).*

__ blank overhead transparency	__ aluminum foil 12" x 12"
__ plain white paper, 8 1/2" x 11"	__ cloth, 12" x 12"
__ metal screen, 12" x 12"	__ plastic screen, 12" x 12"
__ black plastic, 12" x 12" 2–4 mil	__ plastic baggie, 1 gallon size
__ wax paper, 12" x 12"	

For each student:

❑ 1 copy of *Invisible Light Sources, Detectors, and Shields* (master on page 37). (Or use a transparency of the handout as an example to show students and have them draw their own on blank or lined paper.)

For the stations:

Two each of the following stations (see #1 "Getting Ready," page 28)

Station 1—Visible Light
❑ 1 flashlight (with batteries) *[SOURCE]*
❑ 1 plain white paper 81/2 " x 11" *["DETECTOR"]*
❑ 1 *optional:* Set of assorted color filters, such as red, blue, green, to add to shield set

*Please note that in this case the paper only represents the detector. The actual detectors are the students' eyes. The paper reflects the light; our **eyes** are the instruments that detect it.*

Station 2—Infrared Light—heat lamp
❑ 1 infrared bulb with ceramic socket clamp *[SOURCE]*
  [DETECTOR is student's hand]
❑ 1 *optional:* digital camera or video camera *[as DETECTOR]*

Station 3—Infrared Light—VCR/TV remote control
❑ 1 remote control with batteries *[SOURCE]*
❑ 1 TV monitor or other device triggered by remote *[DETECTOR]*
❑ 1 *optional:* digital camera or video camera *[as DETECTOR]*

Station 4—Radio—FM *[SOURCE is radio station]*
❑ 1 FM radio with batteries *[DETECTOR]*

Station 5—Radio—AM *[SOURCE is radio station]*
❑ 1 AM radio with batteries *[DETECTOR]*
  (can use FM/AM radio with FM function disabled by judicious placement of masking tape)

Station 6—Ultraviolet Light
❑ 1 black light—fluorescent *[SOURCE]*
❑ assortment of four or more of the following *DETECTORS:*
  sheet "bright" paper; styrofoam peanuts (5); powdered detergent (about 1/2 oz. in ziplock bag); tonic water containing quinine in a solo cup; index card with UV paint; glow-in-the-dark stars; UV beads.

Black light sources are most often found in party shops or entertainment/theater catalogs. Fluorescent black lights should be used, **not** incandescent black light bulbs. Fluorescent black lights emit far less heat and much more ultraviolet light per watt. Incandescent black light bulbs are **NOT** recommended (see note below).

UV beads are available from Educational Innovations, Edmund Scientific, and many other science education supply houses. The white beads that turn red in the presence of ultraviolet light are preferred. **They work much better in direct sunlight.**

Ultraviolet paint is available from theater supply companies. We have had mixed results with some brands.

SAFETY ISSUES: We strongly advise against the use of incandescent black light bulbs. If that's all you have, be aware that they can become very hot, so caution students **not to touch the bulb**, and they are much less effective in these activities. And although normal fluorescent black lights are considered completely safe, a general precaution is to advise students **not** to stare directly into the fluorescent bulbs for extended periods or from close range. Shorter wavelength black lights used in mineral exploration or to sterilize surfaces should **NOT** be used; they can be dangerous to eyes and skin and can burn them much like a severe sunburn.

Getting Ready

For the infrared station with a remote control as the IR source, a video camera is a big plus as it allows students to see the infrared light coming from the remote control even though it cannot be seen by the eye. This can be one of those "wow" experiences. Video cameras or digital still cameras use light detectors known as CCDs (Charge-Coupled Devices) which are sensitive to infrared light as well as visible light. A "web cam" with computer could also be used. See page 35 for more information and drawings on page 36.

1. Decide how many stations you are going to set up. There are six different stations. For small classes you may only want to set up these six. Having duplicates of all of them (12 in all), if possible, allows students to work in small groups of three students each. You could also set up duplicates of some but not all of the six stations, perhaps those that are more elaborate or may take students longer. Depending on your time constraints, groups can spend 7–10 minutes at each station. If necessary, extend the time over two class sessions.

2. Make photocopies of the student handout, *Invisible Light Sources, Detectors, and Shields* (master on page 37) or make a transparency of it to serve as a model for students to copy.

3. Gather the materials to set up the stations. Make signs to identify the stations by number using the template on page 38, or your own design. Label items so students know how to refer to them on their data sheets. Label the AM radio as "AM Radio," the FM radio as "FM Radio, " the black light as "Ultraviolet," the heat lamp and remote control as "Infrared." Label the envelopes/folders of test shields "Test Shields." Label the TV (or other device operated by the remote control) as "Infrared Detector." Video camera and digital camera can also used as "Infrared Detectors" in this activity. Set up the stations.

4. Read over "Specific Issues/Tips for Invisible Energy Stations" on page 35 to familiarize yourself with issues that may arise. In "Background for the Teacher" at the end of the book, the section on the electromagnetic spectrum may also prove helpful for this and subsequent activities.

Note: There are six different activities. Depending on class size and teacher preference, some teachers set up two of each station (12 in all) or duplicates of several, but not all, of the stations, or just six.

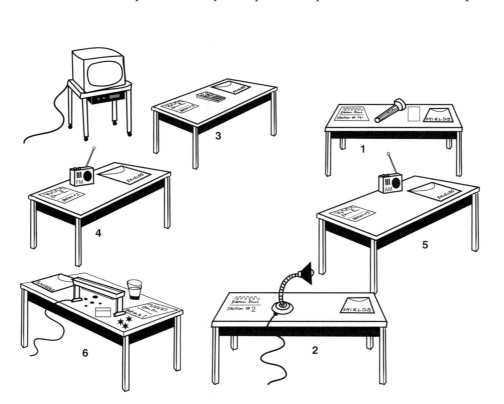

Exploring Invisible Light Stations

Introducing the Activity

Sources of Light

1. Hold up the flashlight (from Station 1), turn it on, and shine it at the students. Say, "This flashlight is a **source of light**."

2. Ask, **"What are some other sources of light energy that we can see?"** Accept several responses. Explain that while most objects *reflect* light to some degree, they are not considered to be the **source** of that light. Sources of light generate and emit the light themselves. They glow and give off their own light. Stars, including our Sun, are sources of light.

3. If students have not mentioned it, point out that the Moon *reflects* the light of the Sun (that's how we are able to see it)—but the Moon is **not** a source of light. We see it and many other objects by reflected light.

Detectors

1. Ask, **"Can you tell me where there are *light detectors* in the room?"** [The students' eyes!—If necessary give them the hint that some light detectors are a couple of centimeters below their eyebrows!]

2. Ask, **"Are there other light detectors that you know of?"** [Cameras, camcorders...]

Transmitters and Shields

1. Explain that some materials let visible light through and they are called **transmitters** of light. You may want to ask students the meanings of the words *opaque*, *transparent*, and *translucent*.

2. Point out that other materials do not let light through; they block the light, and can be called **shields.**

3. Using materials in the "Visible Light" station, show how light can be blocked, or shielded, by a material. Tell them that aluminum foil, for example, could be called a "shield that works" for visible light.

4. Ask, **"What are other things that block visible light?"** [black plastic, paper...]

5. Ask, **"What are some things that don't shield light, but transmit light—that let light through?"** [Glass, clear plastic, water, oil.] Show how different objects can either transmit, partially transmit, or block the light .

Opaque: Not transmitting light; not allowing light to pass through.

Transparent: transmitting light; allowing light to pass through; clear enough to be seen through.

Translucent: admitting and diffusing light so that objects beyond cannot be clearly distinguished; partly transparent.

Station 4

Station 6

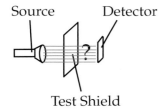

Source   Detector

Test Shield

Some teachers prefer to have the students—as they visit each station—figure out on their own what is the source and what is the detector of invisible light. This is fine, and may be especially appropriate with older students. If you decide to let students do this themselves, then skip this step.

Invisible Energy All Around Us

1. Tell the class that, in addition to the visible light energy they can see in the room, there's a lot of *invisible* energy too.

2. Say there are stations set up around the room, each with a **source** of energy, a **detector** of that energy, and a set of materials as test shields to see which materials may be able to block the invisible energy.

3. Explain that there are six different stations. (If you've made duplicates of any or all of the stations, let them know that too.) Say that the class will work in small groups to investigate Stations #1 through #6 and each student will keep a record of observations on the *Invisible Light Sources, Detectors, and Shields* sheet.

Demonstrate Station Procedure

1. Model the process connected with working at a station, again using Station 1 (visible light).

2. Identify the **source** (flashlight), the **"detector"** (white paper), and the set of test shields. Demonstrate how the test shield material should be placed in between the source and the "detector." In this case, explain that the white paper is being called a detector in that it can reflect the light energy that falls on it and thus allow our eye to see that light. **It is actually our eyes that are the real detectors of visible light.**

3. Use an overhead transparency of the *Invisible Light* worksheet to show where students should make predictions about which materials transmit (T) the light/energy and which ones block/shield (S) the light/energy (in the upper left half of each box). Then show where the observed result is marked (the lower right half of each box).

4. Add that, for the visible light station, making predictions about which materials transmit light and which block/shield it is pretty easy, but with invisible energies, they may be in for some surprises.

Identifying Sources and Detectors

1. **Identify the *Source* and *Detector* at each station.** Go around to each station, hold up the source and the detector, and ask students which is which. As needed, clarify as follows:

Station 1 Flashlight *[SOURCE]*   White paper *["DETECTOR"]*

Station 2 Heat lamp (Infrared bulb) *[SOURCE]*
      Student's hand *[DETECTOR]*
      Optional *DETECTOR*: digital camera or video camera

Station 3 Remote control *[SOURCE]*
      TV monitor (or other device triggered by remote) *[DETECTOR]*
      Optional: digital camera or video camera *[as DETECTOR]*

Station 4 *Radio station [SOURCE]*   FM Radio *[DETECTOR]*

Station 5 *Radio station [SOURCE]*   AM Radio *[DETECTOR]*

Radio Source:

Note: With the radios, it is easy for confusion to arise about the energy source. In addition to the radio waves that are the intended focus of these stations, the radio is powered by electricity (a battery) and there is also sound energy.

Radio Detector:

a. If confusion arises about the radios, ask questions, such as: **"What is the energy source at this station?"** (pointing to one of the stations with a radio). [They will probably say "batteries."] Acknowledge that response but continue on to the next question.

b. Ask, **"Is the sound that the radio makes a type of energy?"** [Yes.] Then ask, **"Where are the signals coming from that provide the sound energy for this radio?"** [A radio station and its transmission tower.]

c. Explain that the **source** of radio waves—the radio tower—is not even in the room, and that the radios, although they *are* a source of sound waves, are NOT a source of radio waves. The information to produce sounds played by the radio is encoded in the radio waves transmitted from the radio tower. **The radio is actually a detector of radio waves.**

Similar to a radio, information to produce sound in a telephone is encoded as electrical or optical (laser light) signals. The encoded signals travel across wires and fiber optics cables and are then decoded at the other end to create the sound emitted by the speaker in the telephone.

Station 6 *Black light [SOURCE]*
    DETECTORS: Sheet "bright" paper; styrofoam peanuts (5); powdered detergent (about 1/2 oz. in ziplock bag); tonic water containing quinine; index card with UV paint; glow-in-the-dark stars; UV beads.

2. Explain to students that the ultraviolet detectors will glow under ultraviolet light because they absorb ultraviolet light (which is invisible) and re-emit it as visible blue light. This is called *fluorescence.*

Ultraviolet paints and glow-in-the dark stars exhibit **fluorescence** *under ultraviolet lights. They also* **phosphoresce**—*they glow for several seconds or minutes after the light is turned off.*

Student Groups Experiment at Stations

1. Divide the class into groups of three students each. If they haven't made their own, pass out a student worksheet to each student.

2. You may want to suggest, as students experiment with the test shields, that they try using several layers of some materials to see if the invisible light still transmits. For example, they could fold a piece of plastic several times or use several thicknesses and see if the infrared light or ultraviolet can still get through. **Caution students to treat fragile items very gently!**

3. Tell students they will have about 7–10 minutes per station. When a given time period is up, have students go to the station with the next highest number, unless they are already on the highest number, in which case they should go to Station 1.

Note: For the radios, make a rule that the station and volume must not be changed. Leave each radio on a low volume and set it on a single station that comes in clearly and is not too disruptive, distracting, or apt to cause students to focus on songs rather than waves! If volumes are set low enough, each radio can be on a different station.

4. At each switch, remind the students to make predictions for each test shield first. You may want to establish a set period of time (e.g. one minute) for prediction-making, during which no one is to touch any of the materials at the station.

5. Circulate and encourage students. You may want to refer to the "Specific Issues/Tips for Invisible Energy Stations" on page 35.

Reflecting on Invisible Light

Discussing Findings

1. Have each group report their results from the last station they worked on.

2. For each station, ask questions, such as the ones below. Encourage other groups to ask questions of the reporting group, and be sure to ask students in the reporting group for any questions they still have.

- **What did you find out?**
- **What was the source?**
- **What was the detector?**
- **What blocked the source?**
- **What let the invisible light through?**
- **Did anything surprise you?**

3. As students respond and discuss, summarize the class experiences on butcher paper or on the overhead so students can view the conclusions and unresolved questions.

Normal water (left) compared with tonic water (right) exposed in UV light.

4. Help familiarize them with the names for each type of invisible light, by asking questions such as:

- **What is the name of the light on the remote control?** [Infrared.]

- **What is the name of the invisible light from the black light?** [Ultraviolet.]

- **What is the name of the light given off by the heat lamp?** [Infrared.]

- **What is the name of the energy that radios detect?** [Radio waves.]

5. Ask, **"What kind of invisible energy do we use to cook with?"** [Microwaves and infrared.] Explain that water is especially good at absorbing microwaves, so any food containing water (most food) will be efficiently heated in a microwave oven. The reason why you're not supposed to put metal in a microwave oven is that the electromagnetic fields in the microwave oven set up extremely powerful electric currents in any material that is a good conductor of electricity, such as metal. Currents can be so strong that the metal rapidly heats up to the point where it literally explodes.

6. Ask, **"What kind of waves are received or transmitted by a satellite TV dish?"** [Microwaves] You may want to discuss circumstances where cell phones don't work—quite similar to circumstances in which radio waves are blocked. (See box at bottom of this page.)

X-Rays and Gamma Rays

1. **X-rays.** Expand the discussion to other areas. Hold up an X-ray image, or put it on the overhead projector. Ask:

- **Where did the rays come from?** the source? [An X-ray machine]

- **Which parts of the body block the X-rays and which let X-rays through?** [Bone blocks X-rays.]

- **How many of you have had a dental X-ray?** When you got the X-ray, they put a lead shield on you. **Why?** [To protect the patient from any dangerous effects from the X-rays.]

- **Why don't they use an aluminum foil shield?** [It doesn't block X-rays! Although aluminum foil blocked all the types of invisible light at the stations, it fails as a shield for X-rays.]

- They had you bite on something. **What was that thing you had to bite down on?** [It held the film (a detector)]

- **What was between the X-ray source and the film?** [Teeth]

The story of Wilhelm Röntgen's serendipitous discovery of X-rays is a fascinating chapter in the history of science. He won the first Nobel Prize for physics for the discovery. See the "Resources" section for several "sources" of more information. It's a great research topic for students!

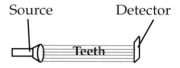

You may want to raise the interesting question of Superman's "X-ray vision" at this point (see the Optional Special Feature on page 34).

2. Let students know that even though people can't see invisible waves, some animals can. We can't see infrared rays, but snakes can. We can't see ultraviolet waves but bees and some other insects can. Can we see radio waves?

3. Remind students that the unit began with a real-life science report about the unexpected discovery of gigantic gamma-ray bursts in outer space. Explain that gamma rays are another type of invisible energy and that people are normally not aware of them. Radio waves, microwaves, infrared, visible light, ultraviolet, X-rays, and gamma rays are different regions in what scientists call the *electromagnetic spectrum.* In the next activity, they will learn a lot more about these regions of the electromagnetic spectrum.

Optional: Microwave Demonstration

Cell phones and pagers operate in the microwave region at wavelengths shorter than FM radio but are hard to block (possibly because they use stronger signals and have error correction circuitry). The signal to pagers and cell phones can be blocked by using metal objects that surround them. Putting a cell phone or pager in a metal file cabinet with all of the drawers shut tightly can work, as can wrapping them in aluminum foil. In either case, there must be not gaps larger than about the thickness of 1 or 2 coins or some of the signal will leak through. Dialing a cell phone or a pager from a nearby phone and seeing if it rings is one way to test whether the signal is being blocked by different objects.

Optional Special Feature: The Superman Dilemma

Superman is actually Kal-El, son of Jor-El and Lara of the planet Krypton. When Krypton blew up in a catastrophic explosion that Jor-El had predicted, Kal-El was a baby. To save their son, his parents put him in a rocket ship to Earth. There he was found and adopted by Jonathan and Martha Kent, who named him Clark, and raised him to be a good citizen and a heck of a nice guy. That's fortunate for us, because as Superman, he can fly very fast, has super strength, X-ray, telescopic and heat vision, acute hearing, a computer-like mind (he can speak all Earth languages and most alien ones) and near invulnerability. Rather than use his powers to impose his will on others, he has chosen to be Earth's gentle guardian, pledging never to kill anyone, or interfere in the free will of nations. There is more information about Superman http://www.batman-superman.com/superman/cmp/superman.html.

1. Ask students about Superman's super powers. If they haven't already mentioned it, ask, **"What is special about Superman's vision?"** [He has X-ray vision—he can see right through things.] (If you wish, give some additional background information about Superman, as given in the marginal note on this page.)

2. Have the class analyze Superman's X-ray vision in terms of what they have just learned about sources and detectors. Ask guiding questions such as:

• **Do people and ordinary objects give off electromagnetic radiation?** [Most things at normal temperatures *do* give off radiation, but it's mostly infrared radiation (heat) that they are giving off. The visible light by which we see most objects is from light that reflects off the objects, *not* light given off by the object. Only at very high temperatures do some things start to glow and give off visible light, for example, a hot tungsten light bulb filament, hot gases in a fluorescent light, or hot gases in the Sun and stars.]

• **Do ordinary objects give off X-rays?** [No, not in any measurable amount.]

• **So how does Superman's X-ray vision work?** [Students may come up with creative ideas here. One possibility is that Superman emits X-rays when he "turns on" his X-ray vision. He always squints his eyes when this is happening. If students bring up this idea, your next questions could be, "So the idea is that Superman turns on a sort of X-ray flashlight that sends out X-rays?" "But if X-rays go right through things and do not reflect off objects, how could those X-rays come back to Superman's eyes for him to see?"

3. To illustrate this dilemma, draw on the board a diagram like the one used in the discussion of dental X-rays. Ask, **"If Superman's eyes are the X-ray detectors, what is the source?"**

4. You may want to conclude by noting that your students' understanding of sources, detectors, and invisible rays has enabled them to question the scientific basis for an alleged Superman superpower that most people assume could exist without thinking about it. It sounds "cool," but doesn't hold up to scientific scrutiny. Of course, anything can be deemed possible in a comic book!

One arguable (if exceedingly unlikely!) explanation is that even though the amount of X-rays given off by ordinary objects is so minuscule that there is no way we can detect them, perhaps Superman can detect that which humans cannot, even with our most sensitive equipment and instruments! In that case, his eyes would indeed be detectors and the "source" would be the exceedingly tiny amount of X-ray radiation given off by various objects.

Specific Issues/Tips for Invisible Energy Stations

Station 3: Remote Control (Infrared)

Image of IR light coming from a remote control unit as captured with a digital camera.

If you connect the camera output to the TV or screen, experiments can be done by aiming the remote control at the camera and putting various objects between the remote control and the camera. The TV or camera screen should face toward the students so they can observe the effect directly. If no video or digital camera is available then use the device controlled by the remote control. For example, the remote control can be used to change channels on a TV, and students can put materials between the remote and the TV to see if they are shields.

A possible source of confusion may result if you set up a station with the TV as an IR detector (sensor for the channel changer) and another station with the TV as a simple display for the digital/video camera. In the first instance the TV is being used as the IR detector receiving the IR signals directly from the remote control device. In the second instance the TV is just a display device for the camera, and as such is part of an IR detector system for which the camera is actually the sensor. This is the kind of ambiguity that is most interesting to raise during class discussion or with individual groups as they encounter the issues. In addition, the TV is also a radio wave sensor!

Some interesting materials mostly transmit infrared, such as black garbage bags (which look opaque to visible light). Solid red phenolic plastic (sometimes used in circuit boards) also seems to be transparent to infrared. Various solid-looking plastics used in clipboards are often transmissive in the near infrared and will amaze students as well. **Simple experiments can also be done at home with the remote in front of the TV.**

Stations 4 and 5: FM and AM Radio

Metal is a good blocker of radio waves. However, since waves can bend around obstacles, the shielding material **needs to cover the radio very completely.** For example, there should be enough aluminum foil to wrap the radio in it. A box could be lined on all sides (including the lid) with aluminum foil. Metal window screen is a good blocker of radio waves, even though it is porous. The gaps between the screen wires are much smaller than the wavelength of radio waves and thus the screen appears solid to the waves! Plastic screens don't have this blocking power. Anti-static bags (such as are used to hold computer parts) are often impregnated with a metal conductive material, and can be good at blocking radio waves. Radio waves generally pass through plastic, unless it has been coated with a coating that conducts electricity.

FM radio utilizes a shorter wavelength than AM radio and is generally easier to block than the AM radio in Station 5. If the AM radio is too hard to block, you might want to tune it to a weaker station. **Battery-operated radios work best as it is hard to block the area around the cords of those that need to be plugged in.**

Station 6: Ultraviolet

A good way to test materials with the black light is to lay the test material on top of the ultraviolet-sensitive beads and then expose the combination to the ultraviolet light source. If the test material is effective at blocking UV light, the beads will not change color.

You may need to dim the lights or close curtains if your room is lit by direct sunlight, in order to see if glow-in-the-dark stars are really glowing. The ultraviolet beads are very sensitive to solar ultraviolet light, and, when outside, turn color immediately on all but the cloudiest days. They turn color when put near **fluorescent** ultraviolet sources, but are much less sensitive to incandescent ultraviolet light (also not recommended for safety reasons).

Going Further

1. Have students continue experimenting with some of the different sources and detectors. How far away can a remote control work? Can it work by reflecting infrared light off other objects? Which objects?

2. With ultraviolet light, measure how many seconds an object will glow after the light is turned off. Measure how far away the ultraviolet light can be from an object and still make it glow. See if there is a difference in response of the UV beads between the artificial UV source and UV in direct Sun.

3. If you have both fluorescent and incandescent ultraviolet sources do experiments to measure their relative outputs and efficiencies. How far away does each one function from the glow-in-the-dark stars? How much energy does each one use? You will probably need to do the experiments in a dark room.

4. Encourage students to research infrared devices used in surveillance, fire fighting, and medicine.

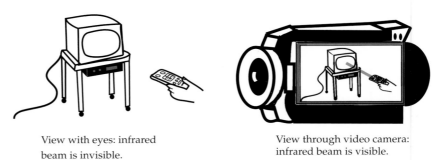

View with eyes: infrared beam is invisible.

View through video camera: infrared beam is visible.

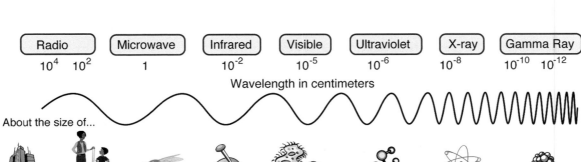

Radio	Microwave	Infrared	Visible	Ultraviolet	X-ray	Gamma Ray
10^4 10^2	1	10^{-2}	10^{-5}	10^{-6}	10^{-8}	10^{-10} 10^{-12}

Wavelength in centimeters

About the size of...

| Buildings | Humans | Honey Bee | Pinhead | Protozoans | Molecules | Atoms | Atomic Nuclei |

Invisible Light Sources, Detectors, and Shields

Code letters: T = Transmitter   S = Shield

Test Shield	Flashlight *Visible Light*	Black light *Ultraviolet*	Heat Lamp *Infrared*	Remote Control *Infrared*	FM *Radio*	AM *Radio*
Clear plastic	prediction / result	prediction / result	prediction / result	prediction / result	prediction / result	prediction / result
Black plastic	prediction / result	prediction / result	prediction / result	prediction / result	prediction / result	prediction / result
Aluminum foil	prediction / result	prediction / result	prediction / result	prediction / result	prediction / result	prediction / result
Paper	prediction / result	prediction / result	prediction / result	prediction / result	prediction / result	prediction / result
Cloth	prediction / result	prediction / result	prediction / result	prediction / result	prediction / result	prediction / result
Metal screen	prediction / result	prediction / result	prediction / result	prediction / result	prediction / result	prediction / result
Plastic screen	prediction / result	prediction / result	prediction / result	prediction / result	prediction / result	prediction / result
Wax paper	prediction / result	prediction / result	prediction / result	prediction / result	prediction / result	prediction / result
Plastic baggie	prediction / result	prediction / result	prediction / result	prediction / result	prediction / result	prediction / result
(other)	prediction / result	prediction / result	prediction / result	prediction / result	prediction / result	prediction / result

Electromagnetic Energy

Region of electromagnetic energy:

Station # _____

Activity 3: Putting the Electromagnetic Spectrum Together

Overview

In this activity, students use their experiences in the previous two activities to place new information about the electromagnetic spectrum into a meaningful context. Electromagnetic Spectrum cards describe each of the major regions of the spectrum—its relative energy, its wavelength, its sources, and detectors. The cards also describe some of the uses that have been made of each region on the spectrum. Student groups are asked to consider the information on all the cards, and then to sort them by whatever characteristics or attributes they choose. This allows students to give free rein to their own creative ways of considering information, before they are introduced to the way scientists generally view it. The main goal of this activity is to encourage the students to continue building their understanding of the electromagnetic spectrum, and to familiarize them with the attributes of different regions. This in turn sets the stage for the astronomy-related uses of the different regions in Activity 4, and a return to the gamma-ray burst mystery in Activity 5.

BIG NUMBER ALERT! There's a huge range of wave sizes in this activity, so you may want to review information on the metric system in "Background for the Teacher" and do some preparation with students on large numbers and their notation. This will also come in very handy for Activities 4 and 5.

What You Need

The Electromagnetic Spectrum Card masters for photocopying, pages 48–57, do not have page numbers because otherwise students might sort by page number!

This excellent video is also available from NASA/JPL Educator Resource Center, 1460 East Holt Ave., Suite 20 Pomona, CA 91767. The phone number is (909) 397-4420. On the Web, the video can be downloaded from http:// ipac.jpl.nasa.gov/webvideo/ video_isdn.html and it also appears on the CD that accompanies the GEMS guide Living with a Star.

For the class:

❏ 2 sets of the ten 8 1/2" x 11" Electromagnetic Spectrum Cards (masters on pages 48–57); one set on card stock and the other set as overhead transparencies.
❏ 1 videotape player, monitor, and NASA JPL videotape: *The Infrared World: More Than Your Eyes Can See*
❏ the sources and detectors from Activity 2, if possible, without any experimental objects and with all devices turned off.
❏ 1 overhead projector

For each group of 4–6 students:

❏ 1 full set of the ten 8 1/2" X 11" Electromagnetic Spectrum Cards on card stock (masters for photocopy on pages 48–57)

For each student:

❏ 1 copy of the homework inventory worksheet, *Invisible Emitters and Detectors* (master on page 47)

Getting Ready

1. For each group of students, make a full 10-card set of the 8 1/2" x 11" cards. (If you have groups of six in a class of 30, you'd make five sets.) *Optional:* Laminate the cards for repeated use.

2. Make a copy of the worksheet, *Invisible Emitters and Detectors*, for each student.

The Parable of the Blind Men and the Elephant

It was six men of Indostan
To learning much inclined,
Who went to see the Elephant
Though all of them were blind,
That each by observation
Might satisfy his mind.

The First approached the Elephant
And, happening to fall
Against his broad and sturdy side,
At once began to bawl:
"God bless me, but the Elephant
Is very like a wall!"

The Second, feeling of the tusk,
Cried, "Ho! what have we here
So very round and smooth and sharp?
To me 'tis mighty clear
This wonder of an Elephant
Is very like a spear!"

The Third approached the animal
And, happening to take
The squirming trunk within his hands,
Thus boldly up he spake:
"I see," quoth he, "The Elephant
Is very like a snake!"

The Fourth reached out an eager hand,
And felt about the knee:
"What most the wondrous beast is like
Is very plain," quoth he;
"'Tis clear enough the Elephant
Is very like a tree!"

The Fifth, who chanced to touch the ear,
Said, "Even the blindest man
Can tell what this resembles most;
Deny the fact who can:
This marvel of an Elephant
Is very like a fan!"

The Sixth no sooner had begun
About the beast to grope
Than, seizing on the swinging tail
That fell within his scope,
"I see," quoth he, "the Elephant
Is very like a rope!"

And so these men of Indostan
Disputed loud and long,
Each in his own opinion
Exceeding stiff and strong.
Though each was partly in the right,
They all were in the wrong!

by John Godfrey Saxe (1816–1887)
from the collection of "Best Loved Poems of
The American People."

*(See another version of this poem
on page 116.)*

GO! The Elephant and the Spectrum

1. Read the poem "The Parable of the Blind Men and the Elephant" out loud to students (or have several students read it). Ask them what they think the meaning of the parable is. Accept all responses. The parable applies to many situations in which people see things from very different perspectives.

2. Tell students that the search for information about the Universe could be compared to the story of the wise men and the elephant. The more ways we can observe the Universe, from different viewpoints, the more we can learn. In the case of the visible and invisible parts of the **electromagnetic spectrum**, the parable also applies. Each part of the spectrum provides a different perspective and different information about our world and beyond our world. Only by using all of the tools we have in science can we begin to form an accurate picture of something.

African Elephant

Photo by Alan Gould

3. Have students recall some of the electromagnetic (EM) waves they investigated in Activity 2. Ask, **"Which animals are sensitive to infrared and ultraviolet waves?"** [Infrared can be seen by snakes; ultraviolet by some insects.]

4. Elicit from students and briefly discuss the main parts of the electromagnetic spectrum (radio waves, microwaves, infrared, visible light, ultraviolet, X-rays, and gamma rays).

5. Divide the class into groups. Explain that you are going to hand out a set of electromagnetic spectrum cards to each group.

Sorting and Classifying

1. Tell students that each group will have the same ten electromagnetic spectrum cards. Let them know they will have 10–15 minutes to sort the cards in any order or way they choose. Encourage them to look at the cards carefully, discuss among themselves a way they want to order all the cards, then arrange them on a desk or table in the order of their sort. **Emphasize that for this activity there is no one "right" way.** They can be **creative** in deciding how they want to order or sort, so long as the entire group agrees with the plan. Tell them that after all groups are finished, each group will get a chance to describe and/or display how they sorted. They may want to have one student be the recorder, and they should plan how to present/display their sorting method(s) to the rest of the class.

Here are a few possibilities of ways to sort: in order by wavelength/energy; in order by harmfulness to living things; in order by "usefulness to people" (subjective); grouped according to those with higher energy than visible light as opposed to those with lower energy than visible light. Students may come up with their own imaginative ways. That's fine!

2. Distribute the cards and have the class begin. Circulate among the groups to make sure they are making progress. If a group is having difficulty you may want to ask them some questions to give them some ideas. If some groups finish quickly, tell them and the class that they could record their first sort and consider coming up with another way.

Some teachers have had student groups circulate to see how other groups sorted.

3. When all groups are finished, reconvene the class and ask each group to report on the way, or ways, they sorted. Allow a chance for full discussion of students' ideas. Group members can describe their sorting approach and display the cards arranged accordingly.

Sorting By Wavelength or Energy

1. Acknowledge all of their sorts or groupings. Then tell the class that a common scientific way is to arrange the cards in order by wavelength, beginning with the longest wavelengths (radio waves) and continuing in order through to gamma rays, at the shortest wavelengths. This order relates to frequency and energy as well.

2. Have student volunteers display a full set of the cards arranged in this order, with radio waves on the left, on the wall or other place visible to the class. Plan to leave this display up for the rest of the *Invisible Universe* unit.

The visible region of the EM spectrum, from about .4 to .7 microns has different colors corresponding to different wavelengths that are (approximately):
violet .42 microns
indigo .44 microns
blue .47 microns
green .53 microns
yellow .58 microns
orange .61 microns
red .66 microns

[a micron is a millionth of a meter]

3. Ask students, **"Did you notice a connection between the length of a wave cycle and the amount of energy?"** Encourage sufficient discussion so students are able to see that it is an inverse relationship—the longer the wave, the less energy; the shorter the wave, the more energy. **"What region has the most energy?"** [gamma rays] **"The least?"** [radio waves.] Point out that a common scientific sort of the spectrum—from the longest wavelength to the shortest wavelength—is the same as sorting from least energy to most energy.

4. Summarize by telling students that this arrangement is called the *electromagnetic spectrum.* All of the waves are electromagnetic energy. They range across the spectrum from lowest to highest energy and have different wavelengths—but they are all electromagnetic energy. They differ in many other ways, including how harmful they are to people and animals, how they can be transmitted and detected, and how they can be useful, but they are all electromagnetic energy.

Astronomical Observations

1. Explain that one important use, among many, for our knowledge of the electromagnetic spectrum is in astronomy. Say that of course we are all familiar with the idea of looking up at the sky, and of using a telescope to see better. Ask, **"What region of electromagnetic energy are we detecting when we use a regular telescope?"** [Visible light.] Explain that modern astronomy has found ways to detect astronomical objects, activity in space, and energy in the Universe in many other wavelengths—not just visible light.

2. Explain to the class that when astronomers observe objects in space by detecting the electromagnetic waves they emit, some of the waves make it through the atmosphere, while other wavelengths are blocked (*absorbed*) by the atmosphere.

3. Ask students to use their cards to respond to the question: **"Which wavelengths are absorbed by the atmosphere?"** [The ones that cannot be detected by ground-based instruments and require space-based detectors on satellites. This includes ultraviolet B, X-rays, and gamma rays.] Have volunteers come up to identify which waves can be observed from the ground and which must be observed from space. You may want to have a student group the card set you've displayed into these two groups.

Even though visible light and other regions of the spectrum do come through the atmosphere, that doesn't mean that visible light detectors should not be put into space. NASA's Hubble Space Telescope, for example, has been able to obtain images not available from Earth as it is much higher up and can look at the skies without the interference of the atmosphere.

4. If you were able to display the sources used in Activity 2, before collecting the Electromagnetic Spectrum Cards ask a group to volunteer to match their cards with the sources at the stations, placing a card next to each appropriate object. They can display cards for X-rays and gamma rays, but without corresponding sources, since there were no X-ray or gamma-ray sources in the activity. (You could have available the X-ray image used earlier.)

The World of Infrared

1. Have the class imagine that they have eyes sensitive to the infrared, in particular to thermal infrared—a rattlesnake is sensitive to this wavelength. Ask, **"What would the world look like through infrared eyes?"**

2. Have students write down their predictions about what the world would look like. Give them the clue that whatever is hotter will look brighter when looking through infrared eyes. Cooler objects will appear darker.

3. Spark ideas for predictions with other questions such as: **"With infrared, what might animals at the zoo look like?" "What would the room look like?" "A car?" "An airplane?" "Your face?" "What would blow-drying your hair look like when seen through infrared-sensitive eyes?" "How would what you see change with the room lights on?" "With the room lights off?"**

4. Allow about five minutes writing time for their responses, then show the video *The Infrared World: More than Your Eyes Can See* (8 minutes).

5. After viewing the video, lead a discussion including these questions: **"What surprised you about how the world looks in the infrared?" "How might infrared eyes be useful in everyday life?" "If this would be useful, why do so few animals have infrared-sensitive senses?"**

6. Emphasize that, just as infrared can be used to provide information that cannot be gained from visible light, so do all the parts of the electromagnetic spectrum provide new information and ways of looking at the Universe. In the next session, they will take a tour of the Solar System, the stars, and outer space, with images derived from many of the different parts of the electromagnetic spectrum. Over time, as scientists put all these observations together—as the men in the elephant parable should have done—people will learn a lot more about the Universe and its many mysteries.

7. As homework, have students make a list of as many objects in their home (or other places) that emit or detect invisible light or waves on the checklist given. Write the name of the object and type of invisible wave using a worksheet like the one on page 47.

Going Further

1. Electromagnetic Riddles. Give students a few minutes to devise a riddle about one of the parts of the spectrum without naming it. For example, "I am a wave that heats up food...the machine goes beep and the food is hot...." (microwave). Encourage discussion, especially if difficult riddles are encountered.

2. Remind students that there are space astronomy observatories that utilize the different regions of the electromagnetic spectrum. Particularly exciting are new gamma-ray missions such as the Swift Mission (see following pages) that are looking for gamma-ray bursts. Have students research one or more of the following projects and scientific investigations.

There is a good website on the electromagnetic spectrum at http:// imagers.gsfc.nasa.gov/ems/ index.html

Space Astronomy Observatories—High Energy

Gamma-Ray Observatories

✛ **Compton Gamma-Ray Observatory (CGRO)**

The Compton Gamma-Ray Observatory, from its launch in 1991 until it re-entered the Earth's atmosphere in 2000, made many discoveries: the mapping of over 2500 gamma-ray burst positions which showed that the bursts could not be localized in our Galaxy; the discovery of a fountain of anti-matter shooting out of the center of our Galaxy; and the discovery that the most prolific type of high-energy gamma-ray source is a type of active galaxy known as a blazar. Blazars are galaxies that contain super-massive black holes that are emitting jets; we see gamma-ray emission from those blazars in which the jets are aimed almost directly at us. For more information, see **http://cossc.gsfc.nasa.gov/**

✛ **The Swift mission.** Launched in November 2004, Swift will study about 300 bursts in its two-year nominal mission, and has the capability to determine the origin of the still-mysterious gamma-ray bursts. Swift is the first mission to focus on studying the newly-discovered afterglow from gamma-ray bursts. When it detects a gamma-ray burst, Swift's rapid re-pointing capability will determine high-precision X-ray and optical positions, relayed to the ground, for use by observers at large telescopes. For more information, see: **http://swift.sonoma.edu/**

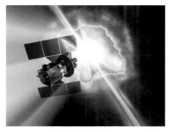

*Swift satellite
Credit: D. Armbrecht
(Spectrum Astro)*

✛ **GLAST, The Gamma-Ray Large Area Space Telescope.** GLAST is a next generation high-energy gamma-ray observatory designed for making observations of very high energy gamma-ray sources. Following launch in 2006, GLAST will study exploding stars, pulsars and jets shooting out of black holes at the hearts of distant galaxies. See **http://glast.sonoma.edu**

X-Ray Observatories

✛ Rossi X-ray Timing Explorer (RXTE) is a satellite that observes the fast-moving, high-energy worlds of black holes, neutron stars, X-ray pulsars and bursts of X-rays that light up the sky. RXTE was launched by NASA in December 1995, and is still taking data from low-Earth orbit. See

http://rxte.gsfc.nasa.gov/docs/xte/xte_1st.html

✛ **ROSAT**, the Röntgen Satellite, was an X-ray observatory developed through a cooperative program between Germany, the United States, and the United Kingdom. It was launched by the United States on June 1, 1990. The mission ended after almost nine years, on February 12, 1999. ROSAT did a complete survey of the X-ray sky, cataloging hundreds of thousands of X-ray sources. See **http://wave.xray.mpe.mpg.de/rosat/mission/rosat**

✛ **Chandra**, NASA's premier X-ray observatory, was named the Chandra X-ray Observatory in honor of the late Indian-American Nobel laureate, Subrahmanyan Chandrasekhar. Since its launch in July 1999, Chandra has been returning spectacular images of the high-energy sky. In fact, Chandra can observe X-rays from particles up to the last second before they fall into a black hole! See **http://chandra.harvard.edu**

Ultraviolet Observatories

✛ **Extreme Ultraviolet Explorer (EUVE):** EUVE was a pioneering NASA mission, which operated from June 1992 through January 2001. It was the first observatory to study the relatively unexplored extreme ultraviolet band. EUVE detected many nearby sources of hot gas, white dwarfs, and a few unexpected sources from outside our Galaxy. For more information, see **http://ssl.berkeley.edu/euve/**

✛ **Far Ultraviolet Spectroscopic Explorer (FUSE)** was launched on June 24, 1999 to explore the Universe in the far-ultraviolet spectral region. Still in orbit, FUSE is seeing hot gas bubbling up out of galaxies and stars, and is studying the distributions of many chemical elements. For more information, see **http://fuse.pha.jhu.edu/**

Space Astronomy Observatories—Low Energy

Visible Observatories

✢ **Hubble Space Telescope**: In its second decade of operations, HST continues to make a huge number of very important observations, and is still returning spectacular images of the visible sky and the UV and IR as well. For more information, see **http://www.stsci.edu/**

Infrared Observatories

✢ **Infrared Space Observatory (ISO)** is a European Space Agency mission launched in 1995. ISO surveyed the infrared sky, studying cool gas, disks around young stars, water vapor and distant galaxies. See **http://www.iso.vilspa.esa.es/**

✢ **Space Infrared Telescope Facility (SIRTF).** One of NASA's Great Observatories, SIRTF is expected to be launched in 2003. It will study some of the coldest objects in the Universe, as well as dusty regions where stars are being born. For more information, see **http://sirtf.caltech.edu**

✢ **Stratospheric Observatory for Infrared Astronomy (SOFIA).** SOFIA is an infrared telescope that will be repeatedly flown in a modified jumbo jet, lofted above the Earth's obscuring atmosphere. The first SOFIA flights are expected to occur in 2004. See **http://sofia.arc.nasa.gov/**

✢ **James Webb Space Telescope (JWST).** The successor to NASA's very successful Hubble Space Telescope, JWST will study the very young Universe, observing the earliest galaxies. JWST will be launched sometime after 2009. For more information, see **http://jwst.gsfc.nasa.gov/**

Microwave Observatories

✢ **Microwave Anisotropy Probe (MAP).** Launched in July 2001, MAP is studying the very small temperature differences in the cosmic microwave background created by the Big Bang, which have led to the formation of large scale structure in the Universe. See **http://map.gsfc.nasa.gov/**

✢ **Cosmic Background Explorer (COBE).** COBE was the pioneering mission that originally mapped the fluctuations in the cosmic microwave background, and measured its black-body energy spectrum. For more information, see: **http://space.gsfc.nasa.gov/astro/cobe/**

Radio Observatories

✢ **Space VLBI.** Space VLBI is an exciting new kind of scientific observation of unusual astronomical objects that requires the simultaneous use of many ground radio telescopes and at least one radio telescope in space. The only Space VLBI to date utilized the Japanese HALCA satellite. This method allows radio astronomers to combine many telescopes located around the world. The acronym VLBI stands for Very Long Baseline Interferometry, a well-established observing technique used by radio astronomers. For more information, see **http://www.vsop.isas.ac.jp/index.html**

Stratospheric Observatory for Infrared Astronomy (SOFIA).

Name: _____

Homework Challenge:

Invisible Emitters and Detectors

Make a list of as many objects as you can in your home or neighborhood that emit or detect invisible light. Write the name of the object and the type of invisible light you think it emits or detects. How many can you find?

Object	Region of Invisible Light	Emits or Detects?
1. TV remote control	infrared	emits
2. TV		emits
TV		detects
3. Radiator		
4. Wireless phone		
5. Radio		
6. Car remote control		
7. Remote controlled car		
8. Microwave oven		
9. Satellite dish		
10. Radio tower		
11.		
12.		
13.		
14.		
15.		
16.		
17.		
18.		
19.		
20.		
21.		
22.		
23.		
24.		

LOW FREQUENCY RADIO

1

Emitted by:
- Sun
- Astronomical objects
- Radio station transmitters for AM radio

Detected by:
- Ground-based astronomical radio telescopes
- AM radios

Radio Image of Sun from the MIT Haystack Observatory
from http://fourier.haystack.mit.edu/urei/tut8.html#8.1

Radio telescope at Goldstone Tracking Center

2

Useful for:
- Radio astronomy
- Listening to music and talk-radio shows

Harmful Effects: None known.

3

Wavelength: 200 to 600 meters
Energy per photon: about one billionth (10^{-9}) the energy of a visible light photon

VERY HIGH FREQUENCY (VHF) RADIO

1

Emitted by:
- Astronomical objects
- FM transmitters

Detected by:
- Ground-based radio telescopes
- FM radios

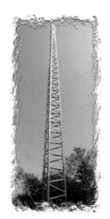

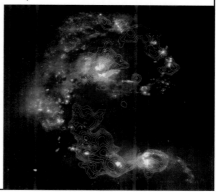

This image has radio contours superposed on a visible-light Hubble image. From Owens Valley Radio Observatory from http://www.ovro.caltech.edu/

2

Useful for:
- Radio astronomy
- Listening to music and talk-radio shows

Harmful Effects: None known.

3

Wavelength: 2.8 to 3.4 meters
Energy per photon: One ten-millionth (10^{-7}) the energy of a visible light photon

MICROWAVE

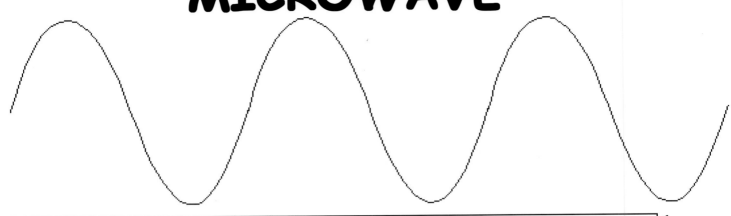

1

Emitted by:
- Gas clouds collapsing into stars
- Microwave ovens
- Radar stations
- Cell phones

Detected by:
- Ground-and space-based microwave telescopes
- Food (heated)
- Cell phones
- Radar systems

Submillimeter radio telescope in Arizona

MAP (Microwave Anisotropy Probe) space telescope

2

Useful for:
- Microwave astronomy
- Cooking
- Radar
- Communications

Cell phone

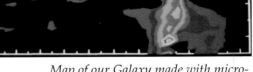

Map of our Galaxy made with microwaves given off by hydrogen

Harmful Effects: At very high intensities, certain wavelengths can heat up living cells and kill them. Cellular phones have been suspected of affecting the brain, but no strong evidence of this has been found.

3

Wavelength: 1 millimeter (mm) to 1 meter
Energy per photon:
One millionth (0.000001 or 10^{-6}) the energy of a visible light photon

THERMAL INFRARED

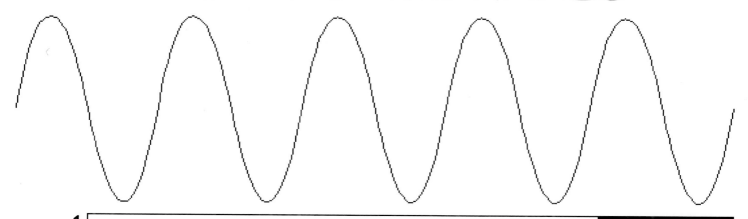

1

Emitted by:
- Food warming lights
- Just about everything at room temperature or above
- Lasers
- Bodies of people and animals

Detected by:
- Infrared telescopes in space and on high-flying airplanes
- Ground-based infrared detectors
- Your skin • Rattlesnakes' eyes
- Night vision devices

A man (right) and a cat (below right) as seen in the infrared

NASA's Stratospheric Observatory for Infrared Astronomy has a large infrared telescope on a modified Boeing 747

2

Useful for:
- Restaurants (heating food)
- Hospitals (sterilization)
- Animal vision
- Security cameras
- Radiant space heaters

Harmful Effects: Very high intensity can heat up living tissues and kill them.

3

Wavelength: 10 microns (or 0.00001 meters or 10^{-5} meters)
(a micron is a millionth of a meter)
Energy per photon: 1/20 the energy of a visible light photon

1 micron = 1 micrometer
= 10^{-6} meter
= .000001 meter

NEAR INFRARED

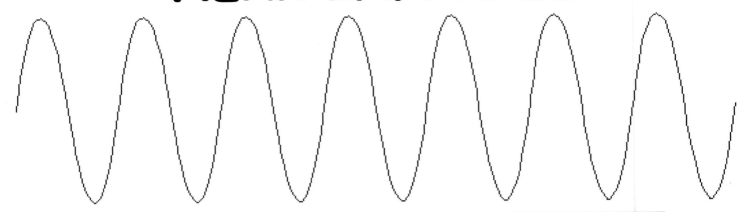

Emitted by:
- Sun and other stars
- TV remote controls
- Computers with infrared ports
- Laser diodes used in fiber optics for telephone communication
- Plants with chlorophyll

Detected by:
- Ground- and space-based infrared astronomy cameras
- TVs • Digital cameras
- Many video cameras
- Printers with infrared receivers, computers

Infrared picture of a typical street scene

1

Useful for:
- Looking for young stars
- Communication in the air
- Communication over optical fibers

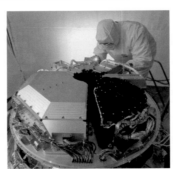

Preparing a satellite equipped with infrared detectors

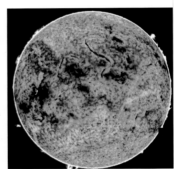

Infrared image of the Sun
from http://solar.physics.montana.edu/YPOP/ Spotlight/Today/infrared.htm

Harmful Effects:
Generally safe, very high intensity can heat tissue.

2

Wavelength: 0.8 to 3 microns (millionths of a meter); smoke particles are about half a micron in size

Energy per photon: about 1/2 the energy of a visible light photon

1 micron = 1 micrometer
$= 10^{-6}$ meter
$= .000001$ meter

3

VISIBLE

1 **Emitted by:**
- The Sun and other astronomical objects
- Laser pointers
- Light bulbs
- Heat lamps in restaurants

Detected by:
- Cameras (film or digital)
- Human eye • Animal eyes
- Plants (chlorophyll absorbs red light)
- Ground- and space-based telescopes and instruments

from http://www.stlukeseye.com/anatomy.htm

2 **Useful for:**
- Solar observations
- Plant growth
- Lasers
- Vision
- Photography

Harmful Effects: Normally harmless, can cause blindness or burn tissue at high intensity (from the Sun or a laser).

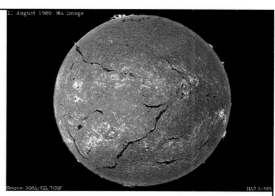

Image of the Sun, taken through a special red filter
from http://www.hao.ucar.edu/public/slides/slide6.html

3 **Wavelength:** about the size of bacteria; 1/2 micron (millionth of a meter) 0.6 micron (red); 0.5 micron (yellow/green); 0.4 micron (blue/violet)
Energy per photon: enough to knock electrons off of some atoms.

1 micron
= 1 micrometer
= 10^{-6} meter
= .000001 meter

ULTRAVIOLET A

1

Emitted by:
- Black light bulbs
- a little by tanning lamps
- UV lamps for rock and mineral identification

Detected by:
- Flying insects, such as house flies
- Black and white film
- Fluorescent paints that are used to convert ultraviolet light to visible colors

from http://www.pestproducts.com/images/

2

Useful for:
- Attracting insects
- Illuminating black light posters
- Mineral identification

Harmful Effects:
In high doses may contribute to skin cancer or eye damage.

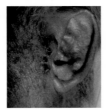

skin cancer (basal cell carcinoma)

Viceroy Butterfly
(Kentucky state butterfly)
http://gov.state.ky.us/symbols/ butterfly.jpg

3

Wavelength: 0.34 to 0.4 microns (millionths of a meter); the size of a small bacteria

Energy per photon: about double the energy of a visible light photon

1 micron = 1 micrometer
= 10^{-6} meter
= .000001 meter

ULTRAVIOLET B

1

Emitted by:
- Tanning booths
- The Sun and hotter stars

Detected by:
- Space-based astronomical ultraviolet detectors
- Ultraviolet cameras

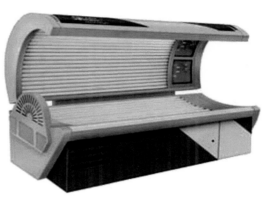

from http://www.novatan.com/store/prodinfo.asp?number=SOL36175-3F&variation=&aitem=1&mitem=2

2

Useful for:
- Studying the Sun and hotter stars
- Tanning (but see below)

Harmful Effects: sunburn and skin cancer

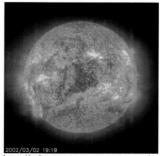

2002/03/02 19:19
http://sohowww.nascom.nasa.gov/

The Sun in extreme ultraviolet light, from SOHO spacecraft, March 2, 2002.

Courtesy of SOHO consortium. SOHO is a project of international cooperation between ESA and NASA.

Note: There is also **Ultraviolet C** (wavelength 0.1 to 0.29 microns—about the length of a virus) which is very lethal to all living things, and can cause extreme skin burns and cancer. It is used in germicidal lamps to sterilize hospital equipment and water.

3

Wavelength: 0.29 to 0.32 microns (millionths of a meter) or 290 to 320 nanometers (billionths of a meter)
Energy per photon: a bit over double the energy of a visible light photon

1 micron = 1 micrometer
= 10^{-6} meter
= .000001 meter

X-RAY

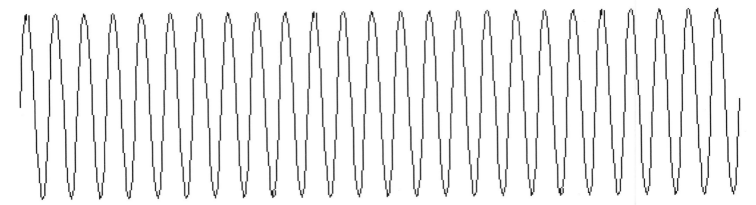

Emitted by:

- Astronomical objects that have temperatures of millions of degrees
- X-ray machines in hospitals
- CAT scan machines
- Older televisions in very low doses
- Radioactive minerals
- Airport luggage scanners

Detected by:

- Space-based X-ray detectors
- X-ray film   • CCD detectors

X-ray: NASA/UIUC/Y. Chu et al., Optical: NASA/HST

Combined X-ray and visible image of Cat's eye planetary nebula

1

Useful for:

- Astronomical observations
- Medical diagnosis
- Security scanning

Harmful Effects:

DNA mutations, high doses can cause death, lower doses can cause cancer.

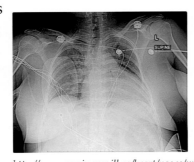

http://www.mmip.mcgill.ca/heart/pages/xr991207r31.html

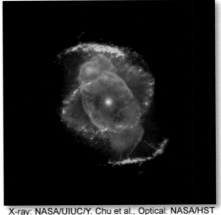

X-ray image of the Sun from the Yokoh satellite
from: http://lasp.colorado.edu/snoe/graphics/solar.html

2

Wavelength: From about the length of a water molecule to the length of a large protein molecule

Energy per photon: from about 1,000 to 100,000 times the energy of a visible light photon

3

GAMMA RAY

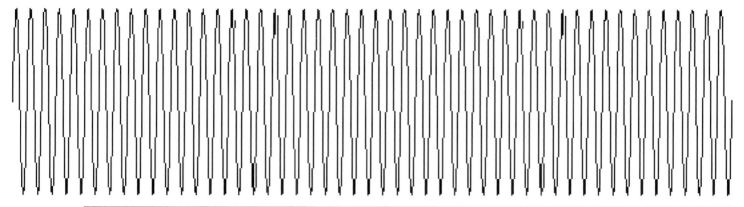

1

Emitted by:
- Radioactive materials
- Exploding nuclear weapons
- Gamma-ray bursts and other astronomical sources
- Solar flares

from http://www.enviroweb.org/issues/ nuketesting/hew/Usa/Tests/Ukgrable2.jpg

Compton Gamma Ray Astronomical Observatory satellite from http://cossc.gsfc.nasa.gov/

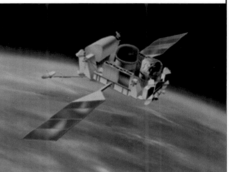

Detected by:
- Gamma detectors on astronomical satellites
- Medical imaging detectors

2

Useful for:
- Studying gamma-ray bursts
- Detecting radioactivity
- Detecting nuclear weapon explosions
- Medical treatments

Harmful Effects: Cancer, radiation sickness.

Hubble Space Telescope image of the visible fireball which accompanied a gamma-ray burst. This image provides evidence that the burst originated in a galaxy seen around the site of the burst.
from http://www.seds.org/hst/gb970228.html

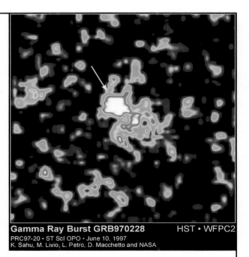

Gamma Ray Burst GRB970228   HST • WFPC2
PRC97-20 • ST ScI OPO • June 10, 1997
K. Sahu, M. Livio, L. Petro, D. Macchetto and NASA

3

Wavelength: 0.001 nanometers and shorter; much smaller than an atom
Energy per photon: more than a million times more energetic than visible light

Activity 4: Tour of the Invisible Universe

Overview

To help you and your students with the astronomy terms used on the Expert's Narration Cards (such as black holes, pulsar, and supernova) there's a concise glossary in the "Background for the Teacher" section.

In this activity, you and your students tour "the invisible Universe." The tour is roughly one-third in our Solar System, one-third in our Milky Way Galaxy (beyond the Solar System), and one-third beyond our galaxy. A worksheet helps keep students actively focused on issues and questions connected with the various tour stops.

The well-known "Powers of Ten" video, originated by Charles and Ray Eames in 1977, would be a great supplement on the concepts of scale and exponential growth. It starts at a 1-meter square image of a picnic, then the camera moves 10 times farther away every 10 seconds, to the edge of the Universe. Then the journey is reversed, ultimately reaching the interior of an atom in the hand of a man. There are now CDs with many new images. For information, contact: http://www.powersof10.com/help/whatis.html

Students often confuse the terms Solar System, Milky Way Galaxy, and Universe. They also do not have a sense of scale about these entities. This session should help them realize that the Solar System is *inside* the Milky Way Galaxy, which is, in turn, inside the Universe. Distances across our Solar System may be measured in millions or billions of kilometers (or miles). Distances across our galaxy are typically measured in light-years—the distance light travels in one year at its fantastic speed of 300,000 km/sec (186,000 mi/sec)! One light-year is about 10 trillion kilometers (6 trillion miles) and our galaxy's diameter is currently estimated at somewhere in the neighborhood of 100,000 light-years! These numbers are difficult for anyone to grasp!

There is a variant of the same idea on the web at: http://micro.magnet.fsu.edu/primer/java/scienceopticsu/powersof10/index.html

This presentation is intended to help students understand the types of objects in the Universe, from more familiar objects in our Solar System to the much more mysterious ones connected with gamma-ray bursts. It also provides dramatic and exciting images derived from detecting the Universe in many different wavelengths on the electromagnetic spectrum.

What You Need

For the class:
❑ 1 set of 12 composite overheads for the *Tour of the Invisible Universe*, showing various astronomical objects (masters on pages 66–77)
❑ 1 overhead projector or computer projector
❑ 1 or more sets of *Expert's Narration Cards for Tour of the Invisible Universe* (masters on pages 63–65)
❑ (*optional*) overhead of gamma-ray bursts (master on page 91). See note on page 60.

Note: Color images of these astronomical objects will be made available for downloading from the GEMS website (www.lhsgems.org)

Optional: Hand out a photocopy of the image description for selected images (or every image) to students interested in helping out with the tour. The student can study the description and when the image comes up in the tour, the student can be the expert on that image and describe it or read the narration.

For each student:
❑ 1 *Tour of the Invisible Universe* worksheet (master on page 62) or blank paper for students to make their own worksheet.

Getting Ready

1. Duplicate the overhead as black and white transparencies, or, preferably, use the color pages in the book to make color transparencies.

2. Decide whether you want students to use the ready-made *Tour of the Invisible Universe* worksheet or make their own. If the former, make copies using the master on page 62.

3. Make copies of and have the Expert's Narration Cards handy. Decide whether you will be doing the narration, or whether you will have students read the descriptions. If students are doing the reading, make enough copies so each student narrator can have his or her own to read. Each group of three students can be responsible for a particular overhead—each has either two or three paragraphs to read, corresponding to "Top," "Middle," and/or "Bottom" images.

GO! Introducing the Tour

1. Explain to the class that they are going to take a tour of the Universe to see what various things look like through the "eyes" of detectors that astronomers use to detect invisible electromagnetic energies.

2. Tell students that astronomers began doing this by using technology to "see" things in X-ray light. Superman aside, these instruments do have "X-ray vision!" Scientists are now going beyond just X-ray images. They are now using detectors for nearly all the wavelengths of visible and invisible electromagnetic energies!

3. Ask students to name some of the astronomical objects that they know. [Take a number of responses.] Jot down some of them.

4. Using the student-generated list, ask which of the objects are:
  • Inside our Solar System
  • Outside our Solar System but inside our Galaxy
  • Outside our Galaxy

Taking the Tour of the Universe

1. During the tour, read yourself, or have students read out loud, the appropriate *Expert's Narration Cards for Tour of the Invisible Universe* about each image. Ask questions to keep the presentation interactive. Encourage students to take notes and jot down questions for further study on each object.

2. Tell students they should write down descriptive words and observations on their *Tour of the Invisible Universe* worksheets, record distances to each object and their relative sizes (if known), and compare images of the same object in different wavelengths.

3. Have students record in the appropriate category: **Nearby** (within the Solar System); **Far** (outside of the Solar System but within our Milky Way Galaxy); and **Really Far** (outside of the Milky Way).

4. Distribute a "Tour of the Universe worksheet to each student.

More detailed tour information may be found on the GEMS website at www.lhsgems.org/iutour.html If students want to pursue any images in greater depth the longer version would be one place to start.

Inquisitive students may well inquire about the process involved in making images we can see that are derived from energies we cannot see. We provide a brief summary in the "Background for the Teacher" section. Computers are used to translate the data gathered by the detectors into images, and colors are assigned to represent different levels of intensity, temperature, energies, etc. Information on what astronomers call "false color" is also in the background information. The Imagine the Universe! website (http:/imagine.gsfc.nasa.gov/docs/teachers/lessons/picture/picture_main.html) includes an activity called "Get The Picture" that simulates the image-making process.

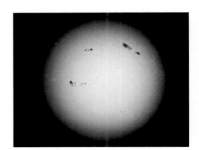

Note: Tour images under #s 1, 2, and 3 are within the Solar System. Images under #s 4, 5, and 6 are within our galaxy (the Milky Way Galaxy). Images under #s 8, 9, 10, 11, and 12 are beyond our galaxy.

5. Begin the "Tour of the Universe," narrating (or having students narrate) asking questions, and encouraging student observations as the tour proceeds.

6. Encourage participation with questions such as: **"What does this look like?" "What do you see?" "What might be causing this to occur?"** Try to keep up a brisk pace that seems right for your class.

Note: We have tried to keep the sample narration concise. If your students' astronomy background and level of interest warrant, you could take the tour again in greater detail, or have interested students pursue a topic in more depth.

After the Tour of the Universe

1. Ask students for their general reactions to the tour and the different images. What did they like the most? Did anything surprise them? Do they have any thoughts about the different ways that visible light, infrared, and X-rays can reveal information?

2. Let students know that these are just a few examples of a vast wealth of astronomy images that have been gathered in recent years. Many of them are now available on NASA and other websites.

On page 91 we have included a page showing actual graphic records of gamma-ray bursts. This page could be made into an overhead and shown during this activity, right at the end of the tour, or right before Step #4 below. These records convey the "burst" nature of gamma-ray bursts in a way that other images do not. It could also be used during Activity 5.

3. Point out that the ability to place telescopes and other instruments on satellites and in space has allowed people to "see" into the Universe as never before.

4. Remind students that several of the images they saw on the tour indicated gamma-ray bursts deep in outer space. Tell them that in the next class session they will return again to the mystery that began the unit and learn more about gamma-ray bursts and their incredible power.

Going Further

You may want to return to the list the class generated during "Introducing the Tour" (page 59) and ask students if any of the objects they named then were on the tour and if any of their earlier estimates of location have now changed.

Ask the class if they know of any comic book super-power heroes (or "she-roes") or villains whose powers are related to invisible rays of any sort. Tell them about the Incredible Hulk (as much or as little as you deem appropriate...) from the "data" on the next page (61).

Gamma Rays and the Incredible Hulk

The Incredible Hulk (the comic book character) was—so the story goes—the result of the accidental exposure of physicist Bruce Banner to gamma rays. This exposure took place during Banner's first test of a "gamma bomb" he invented.

As Hulk fans know, the Hulk's powers are such that he could defeat Superman and Thor with his hands tied behind his back. Hulk can lift approximately 100 tons when calm, but as the old comic book adage tells us, "the Madder the Hulk gets, the Stronger he gets." During times of high stress or anger, an increase in adrenaline causes the Hulk's strength to increase dramatically. There has never been a limit given about the highest strength the Hulk can reach—it is assumed to be without limits. The Hulk held up a 150-billion-ton mountain during the "Secret Wars." He broke open the armor of the dreaded villain Onslaught when the combined might of the rest of the world's heroes couldn't even make a scratch in it!

During the transformation from Bruce Banner to the Hulk and back, he gains and loses large amounts of mass. So much mass is added to the Hulk's leg muscles that he can travel miles in a single casual jump.

The Hulk is immune to all known Earth-based diseases, including AIDS. He has the power of accelerated healing—probably the quickest healing factor of anyone in the Marvel Comics Universe, including Wolverine. The high tensile strength of the Hulk's skin gives him protection from bullets, grenades, shells, and rockets. He can withstand extremely high and low temperatures. He was once deep frozen by "Ice Man" for a long time with no ill effects. He has withstood the vacuum of deep space many times.

For more background on The Incredible Hulk, visit http://io.spaceports.com/~hulk/ or http://www.incrediblehulk.com/

Radiation has also played a role in the origins of other comic book characters, notably Spiderman. In that story, Peter Parker, a high school student, watches a demonstration of radioactivity in a science class. During the demonstration, a spider is accidentally irradiated. The spider bites Peter Parker, and he takes on spider powers! The Spiderman comic was first written at a time when atomic energy was the focus of much science news; the more recent film version shifts the origin to genetic DNA experiments, rather than radiation.

Tour of the Invisible Universe

For each object, check one: (Nearby=Solar System); (Far=in Milky Way Galaxy); (Really Far=outside Milky Way Galaxy)

Object	Nearby	Far	Really Far	Notes/Questions
1. Moon Distance:				
2. Sun Distance:				
3. Jupiter Distance:				
4. Great Nebula in Orion Distance:				
5. Cat's Eye Nebula Distance:				
6. Crab Nebula Distance:				
7. Globular Cluster (M15) Distance:				
8. Supernova 1987A Distance:				
9. Galaxy M51 Distance:				
10. Black Hole Distance:				
11. Gamma-ray Burst 991216 Distance:				
12. The Early Universe Distance:				

Expert's Narration Cards (1–4)
for Tour of the Invisible Universe

1. Moon—Distance: 380,000 km (240,000 miles)

Top: The Moon in Visible Light

This photograph of the full Moon, in visible light, was taken from the Apollo 11 mission, during its trip back to Earth, from a distance of about 18,000 km. The Moon's surface has very interesting features: plains, mountain ranges, and craters. This image includes a portion of the far side of the Moon, never seen from Earth.

Bottom: Moon Eclipsed—Infrared Light

Here's a picture taken from a satellite, using an infrared telescope. It shows a total lunar eclipse in 1997, with the Moon in the Earth's shadow. The bright spots are warm areas on the lunar surface and dark areas are cooler. Infrared light is one of the ways we can find out about temperatures on astronomical bodies.

2. Sun—Distance: about 150,000,000 km (93,000,000 miles)

Top—Visible Light

Some of the most noticeable features on the Sun when viewed with visible light are sunspots. These are magnetic disturbances on the Sun. They look dark because they are "cooler" than the surface temperature of the Sun, if you can call 3,800°C cool! The surrounding surface is about 5,800°C! So sunspots are about 2000° "cooler."

Middle—Infrared Light

This image shows more detail than visible light. Sunspots are seen, but also prominences—they look like tongues of flame at the edge of the Sun.

Bottom—X-ray

When the Sun is viewed in X-rays, larger solar features become evident. Some of these, sometimes called "holes" are not like holes in the ground but are magnetic holes through which a much faster solar wind can flow. Solar wind is the steady stream of particles pouring out of the Sun every second.

3. Jupiter—Distance: about 400,000,000 km (250,000,000 miles)

Top—Visible Light

When 17th-century astronomers first turned their early telescopes toward Jupiter, they saw a large reddish spot on the giant planet. This Great Red Spot is still in Jupiter's atmosphere, more than 300 years later. It is a vast storm, spinning like a cyclone with winds at about 270 mph. The Red Spot has a diameter almost twice the size of Earth.

Middle—Radio Image

This radio image, from the U.S. National Radio Astronomy Observatory, shows a bright central region due to radiation from charged particles trapped in Jupiter's magnetic field.

Bottom—X-ray Image

This Chandra X-ray Observatory image of Jupiter shows concentrations of X-rays near the north and south magnetic poles that pulsate about every 45 minutes. One possible explanation for this puzzling behavior is that ions—particles from the Sun—are captured in Jupiter's magnetic field, and accelerated toward Jupiter's magnetic poles. The ions could bounce back and forth in the magnetic field, from north to south pole in 45-minute oscillations.

4. Great Nebula in Orion (M42) Distance: 1,400 light years

Top—Visible Light

This gigantic gas cloud or Great Nebula is one of the "closest" star-forming regions to Earth. It has many solar systems forming within it. The most abundant gas is hydrogen—the gas that most stars are made of.

Middle—Infrared

Infrared light is excellent for seeing the gaseous parts of the Great Nebula of Orion. Near the center is a star cluster, often called the Orion Trapezium, a cluster of very young stars. These young stars have an average age of "only" 300,000 years! The Trapezium is at the end of Orion's sword.

Bottom—X-ray

This X-ray image is a close-up view of the Trapezium. The X-rays are produced in the multimillion degree upper atmospheres of the stars. Several stars are still surrounded by disks of material that could lead to planetary formation, such as the blue object on the lower left.

Expert's Narration Cards (5–8)
for Tour of the Invisible Universe

5. Cat's Eye Nebula (NGC6543)
Distance: 3,000 light years

Top—Visible

This is a dying star throwing off shells of glowing gas. This Hubble Space Telescope image reveals a very complex structure that makes astronomers suspect the visible central star may actually be a double star system. The term planetary nebula is misleading. Although they may appear round and planet-like in small telescopes, high resolution images reveal them to be stars surrounded by cocoons of gas.

Middle—Infrared

This image was taken with the European Space Agency's Infrared Space Observatory, ISO. Different wavelengths of infrared reveal different features. In this image, 12.8-micron infrared light is from charged neon atoms and shows the planetary nebula elongated by jets from the poles of the star.

Bottom—X-ray

This X-ray image, taken with the Chandra X-ray satellite, shows a bright central star surrounded by a cloud of multi-million-degree gas. The star will collapse into a white dwarf star in a few million years.
All three images are approximately at the same scale.

6. Crab Nebula   Distance: 6,500 light years

Top—Visible Light

In the year 1054 A. D., Chinese astronomers were startled by the appearance of a new star so bright it was visible in broad daylight for several weeks! Today, the Crab Nebula is at the location of that violent exploding star, which was a supernova. The nebula surrounds a neutron star, so dense that it has more than the mass of our whole Sun crammed into a sphere only about 16 km (10 mi) across. A teaspoon of neutron star material, if brought to Earth, would weigh about 1 billion tons!

Middle—Infrared

The nebula is over one light year in size, more than 1000 times bigger than our Solar System. The bright dot in the center of the infrared image shows the size and location of the X-ray image.

Bottom—X-ray

This image is taken with the Chandra X-ray Observatory. The neutron star (pulsar) is spinning 30 times a second emitting pulses of radiation. X-rays are produced by high-energy particles spiraling around magnetic field lines in the Nebula.

7. Globular Cluster (M15)
Distance: 34,000 light years

Top—Visible Light

This stellar swarm of hundreds of thousands of stars is one of a couple of hundred globular star clusters surrounding the Milky Way Galaxy. Globular clusters are believed to be very old—12 billion years old or more. This is one of the largest—about 120 light years in diameter.

Bottom—X-ray

Revealed in this Chandra X-ray satellite image are two neutron binary stars. Previously, astronomers had never seen more than one of these neutron star binaries in any given globular cluster. The X-ray binary star contains a city-sized neutron star orbiting a "normal living" hydrogen-burning star, slightly smaller than our Sun. Escaped gas from the normal star falls onto the neutron star, attracted by its strong gravity. The transfer of gas glows hot when viewed in X-rays.

8. Supernova 1987A
Distance: 168,000 light years

Top—Visible Light

This is an image of Supernova 1987A, taken in 2000 by the Hubble Space Telescope. The supernova was first seen on February 23, 1987. That evening in Chile, a young Canadian astronomer was photographing a nearby galaxy with a small telescope. He developed his film and immediately noticed a bright star where none had been seen before. News sped around the world of this nearby supernova—the brightest one seen since 1604!

Middle—Radio

This is a radio image of Supernova 1987A, from the Australia Telescope Compact Array, taken in 1999. The amazing event occurred in our neighboring galaxy, the Large Magellanic Cloud, in a region rich in young, blue stars. It was one of these stars that destroyed itself in the explosion astronomers call a supernova. The ring glows at radio wavelengths as the shock wave from the explosion hits gas that was expelled from the star over 20,000 years earlier.

Bottom—X-ray and Visible

This Chandra X-ray image, made in 1999, shows the expanding shell of hot gas in the shock wave produced by the explosion. The colors represent different intensities of X-ray emission. On the bottom right is an interesting image from the Hubble telescope showing a triple-ring system of gas around the supernova. The central ring is slightly outside the rings shown in the radio and X-ray images, and is the same as the ring shown in the top visible light image. Scientists expect more brilliant light shows from continuing impacts of the explosion.

Expert's Narration Cards (9–12)
for Tour of the Invisible Universe

9. M51 (The Whirlpool Galaxy)
Distance: 37 million light years

Top—Visible Light. The "Whirlpool Galaxy" is a spiral galaxy, with a smaller companion galaxy nearby. This image is one of many taken by students around the world in the Telescopes in Education (TIE) program.

Middle— Infrared. These are three different infrared images. The near-infrared and mid-infrared images are quite similar to the visible light image and trace the pattern of spiral arms. In the far-infrared, the arms are not as clear, but this wavelength is good for mapping the distribution of dust in galaxies. Dust and gas are the materials from which stars are born, and this galaxy is rich in star-making materials.

Bottom—Radio (left); X-ray (right). These are radio and X-ray images of the Whirlpool Galaxy. The radio image shows the same distribution of light as in the other images. There is a red blob at the end of the southern spiral arm, which astronomers think may be a background quasar. On the X-ray this same area is seen as a small yellow peak.

10. Black Hole Causes Jet in Galaxy M87
Distance: 50 million light years

Top—Visible Light
This Hubble Space Telescope observation shows that the core of Galaxy M87 contains a super-massive black hole. A black hole is an object so massive and compact that nothing can escape its gravitational pull, including light. The object at the center of M87 fits that description—it weighs as much as three billion of our Suns, but is concentrated in a space no larger than the Solar System.

Bottom—X-ray, Radio, Visible
Chandra X-ray Observatory gives astronomers a detailed look at the X-ray jet blasting out of the nucleus of M87, a giant elliptical galaxy. The X-ray image of the jet has an irregular, knotty structure. At the extreme left of the image, the bright galactic nucleus, harboring a supermassive black hole shines. The jet is thought to be produced by strong electro-magnetic forces created by matter swirling toward the supermassive black hole. These forces pull gas and magnetic fields away from the black hole along its axis of rotation in a narrow jet.

11. Gamma-ray Burst (GRB991216)
Distance: several billion light years

Top —Visible Light
This image is an optical view of the area around gamma-ray burst GRB991216 (December 16, 1999). Astronomers are seeking to learn more about these mysterious and powerful explosions. For a brief moment, the light from this blast was equal to the radiance of one million galaxies! By the time this image was taken, the object had already faded to a millionth of its original brightness. The after-glow of the fading GRB fireball is indicated with an arrow. The letters are known stars, which provide a reference point to compare the brightness of the burst to the brightnesses of the stars.

Bottom—X-ray
One scientist said, "The energy released by this burst in its first few seconds staggers the imagination." It released hundreds of times more energy than an exploding star, a supernova. We used to think supernovas were the most powerful energy release in the Universe. Not any more! Some gamma-rays bursts may be the result of a "hypernova," a gigantic star collapsing on itself under its own weight.

12. The Early Universe (Hubble Deep Field)

Top—Visible Light
Several hundred galaxies, many of them several **billion** light years away from us, are visible in this "deepest-ever" view of the Universe, made with the Hubble Space Telescope. There is an awesome variety of galaxy shapes and colors. Some of the galaxies may have formed near the beginning of our Universe. Looking at such distant objects is like looking back billions of years in time, since that is how long it takes to their light to reach us!

Bottom—X-ray
This image shows an X-ray survey of the Hubble Deep Field. The objects that are emitting the X-rays detected provide a deep look into the early Universe. This image is thought to include a central giant black hole, three elliptically-shaped galaxies, an extremely red distant galaxy, and a less distant spiral galaxy.

1. Moon

Visible

Full moon as seen from NASA Galileo spacecraft

Infrared

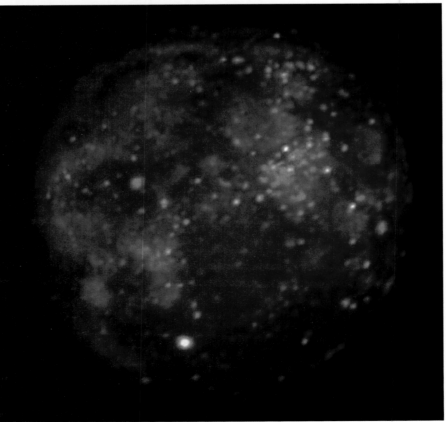

Midcourse Space Experiment (MSX) Satellite

GEMS Tour of the Invisible Universe

2. Sun

Visible

Infrared

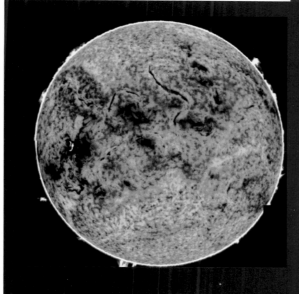

X-ray

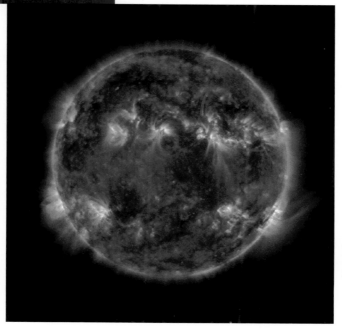

3. Jupiter

Visible

Credit: NASA, 1979.

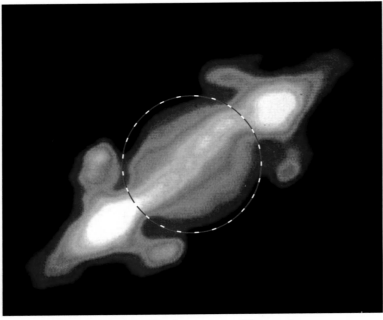

U.S. National Radio Astronomy Observatory

Radio

X-ray

Credit: NASA/CXC/SWRI/G.R. Gladstone et al

GEMS Tour of the Invisible Universe

4. Great Nebula in Orion

Visible

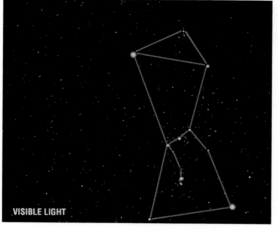

Note: Light blue lines show the constellation of Orion.

Infrared

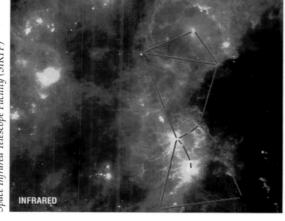

Credit: NASA, Space Infrared Telescope Facility (SIRTF)

X-ray

Chandra X-ray Observatory Center

5. Cat's Eye Nebula

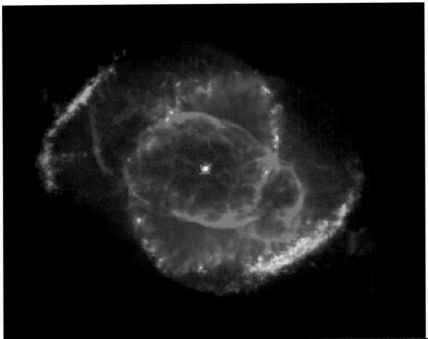

Visible

NASA, Hubble Space Telescope

Infrared

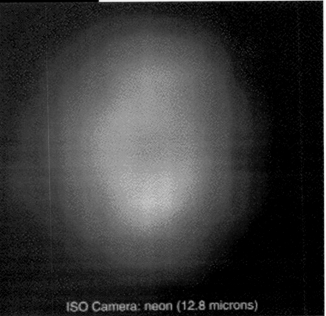

ISO Camera: neon (12.8 microns)

ESA/ISO, CEA Saclay and ISOCAM
Consortium

Chandra X-ray satellite

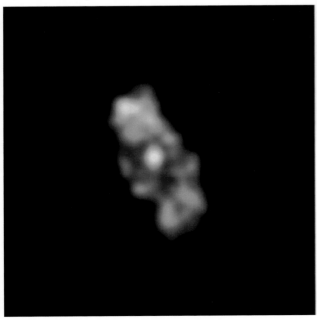

X-ray

GEMS Tour of the Invisible Universe

6. Crab Nebula

Visible

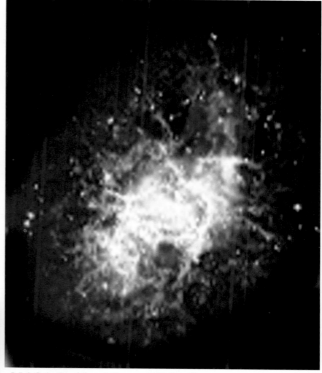

NASA Goddard Space Flight Center

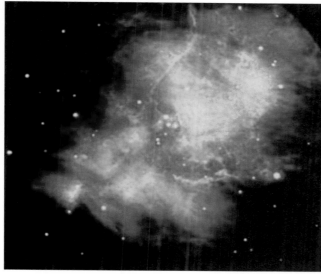

Keck Telescope

Infrared

X-ray

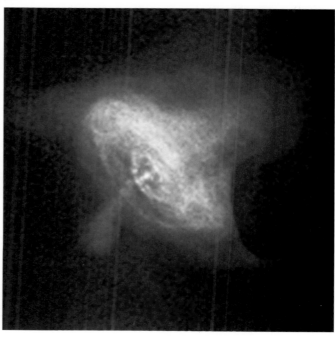

Chandra X-ray Observatory Center
Harvard-Smithsonian Center for Astrophysics
http://chandra.harvard.edu

7. Globular Cluster (M15)

Visible

The Electronic Universe Project
http://zebu.uoregon.edu/messier.html

X-ray

Chandra X-ray Observatory Center
Harvard-Smithsonian Center for
Astrophysics
http://chandra.harvard.edu

8. Supernova 1987A

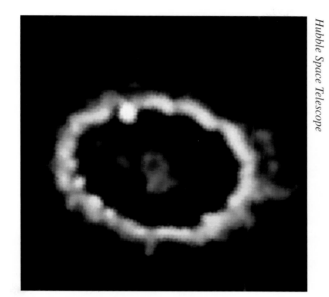

Hubble Space Telescope

Visible

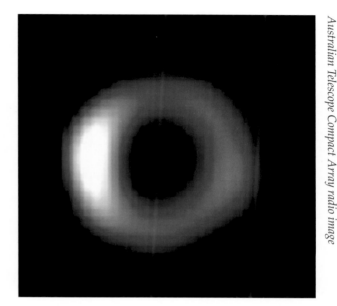

Australian Telescope Compact Array radio image

Radio

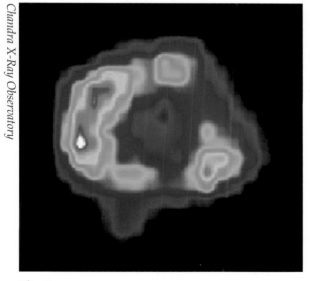

Chandra X-Ray Observatory

X-ray

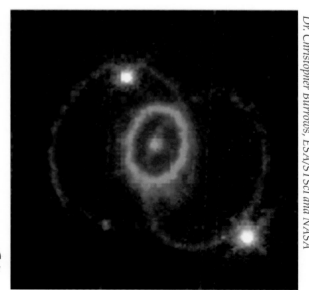

Dr. Christopher Burrows, ESA/STScI and NASA

Visible

9. Galaxy M 51 (The Whirlpool Galaxy)

All these images appear at http://sirtf.caltech.edu/Education/ Messier/m51.html

Visible

Telescopes in Education (TIE), Mount Wilson Institute and Jet Propulsion Laboratory

Two-Micron All-Sky Survey (2MASS)

Near Infrared

InfraRed Astronomical Satellite (IRAS)

Mid-Infrared

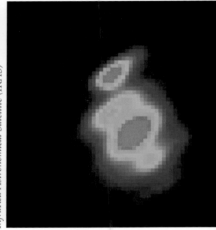

InfraRed Astronomical Satellite (IRAS)

Far-Infrared

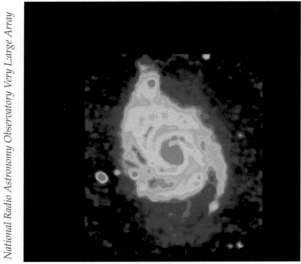

National Radio Astronomy Observatory Very Large Array

Radio

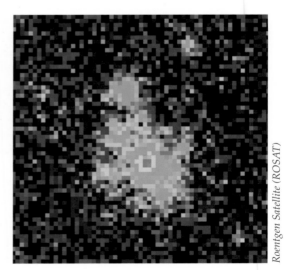

Roentgen Satellite (ROSAT)

X-ray

10. Black Hole/Jet in Galaxy M87

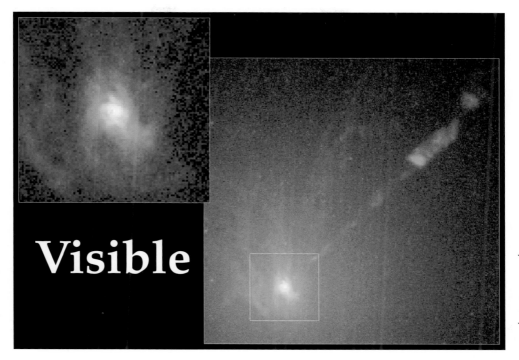

Visible

Hubble Space Telescope

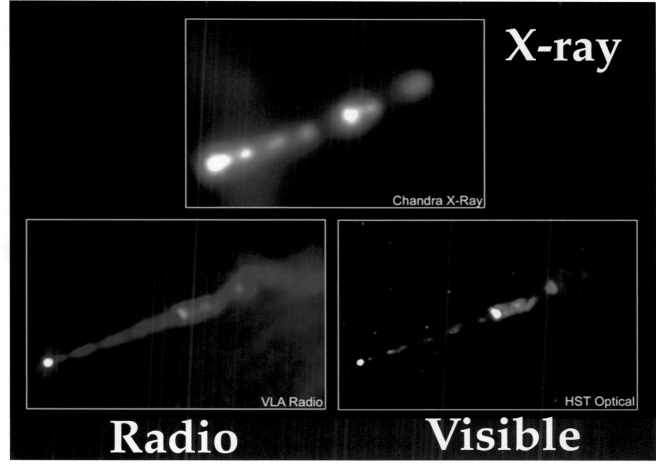

X-ray

Chandra X-Ray

VLA Radio

HST Optical

Radio

Visible

11. Gamma-ray Burst 991216

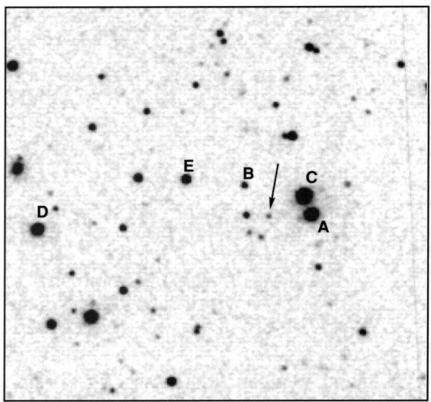

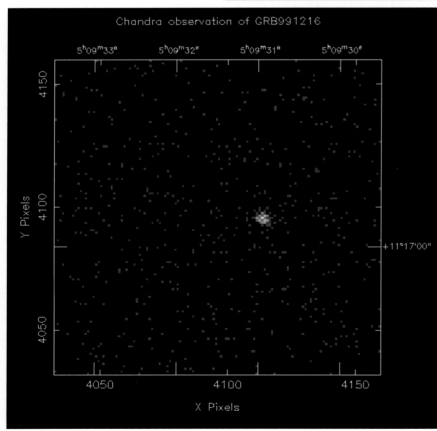

X-ray

Chandra X-ray Observatory Center
Harvard-Smithsonian Center for Astrophysics
http://chandra.harvard.edu

GEMS Tour of the Invisible Universe

12. Early Universe

Visible

Hubble Deep Field — HST · WFPC2
PRC96-01a · ST ScI OPO · January 15, 1996 · R. Williams (ST ScI), NASA

X-ray

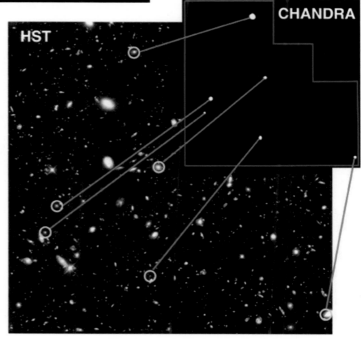

Activity 5: The Most Powerful Explosions in the Universe!

Overview

In this closing activity, students bring understandings gained over the course of the unit to the mystery of gamma-ray bursts. At the start of the unit, a brief dramatic dialogue introduced them to the way gamma-ray bursts were first detected. Over the course of investigating waves and wavelengths, experimenting at the invisible energy stations, and learning about the electromagnetic spectrum, they gained important physical science and astronomy knowledge. They have also seen indications of gamma-ray bursts in the "Tour of the Universe," and learned that they are the most powerful bursts of energy in the Universe today. All of this provides a foundation for a closer look at the most energetic part of the spectrum—gamma rays and the mystery of gamma-ray bursts.

First, a student reading provides some information on recent scientific history relating to gamma-ray bursts. Then, in a series of graphing activities, students compare the power associated with sources of energy on Earth with astronomical sources, including gamma-ray bursts. Students create posters or other graphic representations of what they have learned. The poster assignment can also be used as an assessment activity. Students also learn about the NASA Swift mission, which seeks to find out more about the mystery of gamma-ray bursts, and which sponsored this guide!

What You Need

For the class:
❑ 1 overhead transparency of each of the following: *How Much Energy is That?* (master on pages 84–85); *How Much Energy is in a Gamma-Ray Burst?* (masters on pages 86–88); and *Meteor Crater and Hiroshima* images (master on page 89).
❑ 1 overhead projector

For each student:
❑ 1 copy of the *How Much Energy is in a Gamma-Ray Burst?* student worksheet (masters on pages 86–88)
❑ 1 copy of the article entitled *The Mystery of the Gamma-Ray Bursts* (master on page 90)

Getting Ready

1. Make transparencies and duplicate worksheets.

2. Consider whether a brief review of large numbers and distances, including the metric system, would be helpful. Some resource material has been provided in the "Background for the Teacher" section.

3. Read over other relevant portions of the background section, especially information related to gamma rays and gamma-ray bursts. We've also included an excerpt on gamma rays as a note on the next page.

The Mystery of the Gamma-Ray Bursts (GRBs)

1. Remind students of the "News Flashes" that began the unit. Ask if they remember how gamma-ray bursts were first detected. [During monitoring for bomb test violations.] Tell students that based on all they have learned, they are now ready to learn more about gamma rays and gamma-ray bursts, and to find out how scientists are working to solve the mystery of where gamma-ray bursts come from.

2. Remind them that gamma-ray bursts are the most powerful explosions of energy known in today's Universe. Since they were first detected, another incredible fact has emerged—these flashes are now detected on average about once a day!

3. Hand out *The Mystery of the Gamma-Ray Bursts* article to each student and have them read it in class, taking brief notes, and writing down questions that they have. (If you prefer, the class could read it aloud.) Then discuss the article. Encourage students to ask questions about it. Acknowledge how much students have learned, as compared to when they first heard about the mystery!

4. Tell students that the power of one of these gamma-ray bursts is so gigantic that it is very hard for people to imagine. One way to get a sense of this power is to compare it to other things. They will start by graphing the power of a series of events and compare their power to the power of a gamma-ray burst.

Graphing Powerful Events

1. Distribute the three-page student graphing worksheet *How Much Energy is in a Gamma-Ray Burst?* to each student.

2. Project the first page of the two-page *How Much Energy is That?* transparency. **Use a piece of paper to cover the answers on the right side, so you can uncover them one by one.** Mention that instead of using a scientific measure of energy, the power is first measured in the amount of energy released by a high explosive, such as TNT. Tell them that a pound of TNT releases a great deal of energy.

3. Have students estimate (or guess) what the amount of energy would be for the first event (car crash), then reveal the amount. Do the same for the second (construction site blast), asking for predictions, then revealing the amount of energy.

4. Now focus student attention on the graphing sheet.

Graph A

1. Use the overhead transparency of *How Much Energy is in a Gamma-Ray Burst? (I)—(the first page)* to show students where to write the energy value in the box and how to fill in the thin bar up to that value.

Gamma Rays

Some students may ask or need a reminder about what gamma rays are (which they learned something about as part of the electromagnetic spectrum). Here is an excerpt from the background information:

Gamma rays have wavelengths of less than about ten trillionths of a meter. They are even more penetrating than X-rays. Gamma rays are generated by cosmic objects, radioactive atoms, in nuclear explosions, and are used in medical applications. Gamma-ray bursts are also seen in space, which could be due to the collapse of a supermassive star, or perhaps the combination or merger of two very dense compact objects such as neutron stars. In each case, the end result is thought to be the birth of a black hole. Images of our Universe taken via detection of gamma rays yield important information on the life and death of stars, and on other cataclysmic processes in the Universe.

In scientific measure, the explosion of 1 ton of TNT is equal to about 4.2 billion Joules, or 4.2×10^9 Joules. For more on units of energy and their conversion, see pages 104 and 105 in "Background for the Teacher."

Hiroshima, after atomic bomb

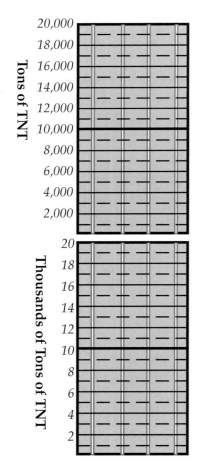

Two of the possible choices for y-axis labels on Graph B.

2. As you demonstrate on the overhead, have students use a pencil to fill in the thin (unshaded) bar on Graph A , only a tiny bit to represent ounces of TNT and write in the energy value in the box below "car crash," (i.e., write in "oz. of TNT"). Do the same for the construction site blast. Say they will continue to make a bar graph for larger events.

3. Put *How Much Energy Is That?* back on the overhead, with just the two events you've done so far revealed. Then, one by one, continue having students make predictions for each event. After each prediction, reveal on the overhead the energy associated with that event and have students record the number in the appropriate box and fill in the thin bar for the event up to the appropriate value on Graph A.

4. When you get to the "Large Quarry or Mine Blast" students may notice that they have reached Graph A's limit. When you next reveal the "Small Nuclear Weapon," ask, **"We're nowhere near the energy of a gamma-ray burst—how can we continue graphing for larger energy events?"** [Make a new graph with a new scale.]

Graph B

1. To "carry over" the power of the biggest "blast" on Graph A, have students rewrite the energy value of a "Large Quarry or Mine Blast" on Graph B, in the box at the lower left. Tell them that soon they will need to determine what units and what scale to use for Graph B.

2. Continue revealing events and having students make predictions about their power. After each prediction, reveal the energy associated with the event and have students record the number in the appropriate box of Graph B, but do not have them fill in the bar, since the scale has not yet been determined.

3. When you get to the Hiroshima A-bomb event, show an overhead transparency of the devastated city for students to gain a visual sense of the amount of the energy released in that horrendous event.

4. Once you have revealed the energy of the "Hiroshima A-bomb," and students have recorded it in the box, ask, **"What scale should we use now for Graph B, to fit the biggest energy event on the scale?"**

5. Explain that this question actually has two parts: (a) **"What units should be used to put in the blank space next to 'Energy in _____'?"** and (b) **"What actual numbers do we write by each horizontal line that can accommodate the number 15,000 tons of TNT, the value of the largest energy event?"** Have students discuss this question in small groups, then have groups suggest their answers to the class.

Note: Students may grapple with this, but eventually they should figure out that the unit to write in must be in "Tons" of TNT, though they might also choose "Hundreds of Tons" or "Thousands of Tons." (As in the sample diagrams on this page.) As far as what numbers to put in the scale, let the class choose, but it's best if you achieve consensus and have everyone use the same units. One logical choice is to label each solid line as multiples of 2000 tons—that will give a maximum scale value of 20,000 tons, which will fit the 15,000 tons required to put the A-bomb event on this graph.

6. Students can now fill in the bars of Graph B, so ask them to do so. Once they are done, have them take note of how the largest energy event on Graph A is now just a dot on our new scale of Graph B!

7. Now, they are again faced with the same challenge as they had when they got to the "Large Quarry or Mine Blast," so again ask **"We are *still* nowhere near the energy of a gamma-ray burst—how can we continue graphing, for even larger energy events?"** [Make another new graph with a new scale.]

Graphs C and D

1. Have the students rewrite the value of the energy in a "Hiroshima A-bomb" on Graph C in the box at the lower left. As before, they will need to determine what units and what scale to use for Graph C.

2. Continue having students make predictions and recording the energy associated with each event, but do not have them fill in the bars, since the scale for Graph C has not yet been determined. When you get to the Meteor Crater, Arizona event, show the overhead transparency of the crater to give students a visual impression of that event.

3. When you get to "Solar Energy received by Earth," it's again time to determine an appropriate scale, so ask, **"What scale should we use now for Graph C?"** [Since "Energy Received by Earth" per second is equivalent to 50 Megatons of TNT per second, an appropriate scale would be "Megatons" of TNT or "Millions of Tons" of TNT. A fairly obvious numbering scheme for Graph C is shown on this page.]

4. Have the students fill in the bars on Graph C, and as before, have them take note of how the largest energy event on Graph B is now minuscule on our new scale of Graph C.

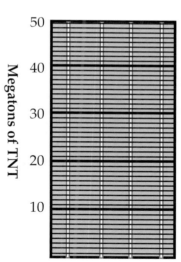

5. For Graph D, have students proceed as before, rewriting the "Solar Energy received by Earth" per second in the first box, predicting and recording values, then determining an appropriate scale. Since the "Chilean Earthquake" is the maximum energy event on Graph D, at 32,000 Megatons of TNT (or 1,000 H-bombs), convenient labels for Graph D would be either "Thousands of Megatons" of TNT or "H-bombs." You may let the class choose which units they would like to use, but it's best if you achieve consensus and have everyone use the same units. Depending on which units are chosen, examples of convenient labels for each **solid** line would be multiples of 100 H-bombs or multiples of 4,000 Megatons TNT.

The Most Powerful Events in the Universe

In an effort to find the best way to communicate the massive power of gamma-ray bursts to students in an accessible way, this activity intentionally shifts the terms in which successive events are described. In physics, power is defined as energy over time (p = e/t). You may want to point this out. By the end of the graphing activity students become aware that—in just a few seconds— a gamma-ray burst sends out many times more energy than our Sun has emitted over the five billion years of its lifetime so far!

1. Tell the students that the next few stages of events are so gigantic that it becomes pointless to graph them, so they will just make predictions and record the actual power on the third page of their worksheet. If the students have not already chosen to switch to "H-bombs" as a unit in Graph D, say they now should do so for the next couple of steps. You may want to have them invent a term for "1 million H-bombs."

2. When you get to the "Supernova Exploding Star," point out that the unit of energy must again change to *"the total output of the Sun during its entire 10 billion year lifetime!"*— that's the energy a supernova puts out in a matter of just days! Then the power of gamma-ray bursts is expressed in number of supernovae.

3. Ask students, **"Why do you think the units changed to total lifetime output of the Sun, instead of using tons of TNT as an energy unit?** [The power of a supernova and a gamma-ray burst are so gigantic that numbers of tons of TNT would go so high that some would have over 30 zeroes!]

4. Point out that each of these last steps is mind-boggling not only in the amount of energy involved, but also in the short periods of time over which the energy is released. Some gamma-ray bursts last thousands of seconds; others last only milliseconds! Allow time for this to sink in. Ask students if they have any comments or questions.

5. Point out that the amount of power in gamma-ray bursts is amazing, and that is certainly one important clue in the unsolved mystery of gamma-ray bursts.

6. Ask the students, **"What do you think might be causing such incredibly powerful events, that can release the energy of trillions of Suns in a matter of minutes or even seconds?"** [Accept several responses] Let students know that the only events and phenomena we know about in the Universe that could generate that much energy are what we think happens when stars and galaxies go through massive changes, as when black holes are formed, or when other incredibly gigantic events and changes take place. We can hardly begin to imagine such events, but gamma-ray astronomy (and astronomy in all the other available wavelengths) is trying to find out more!

The Astronomer and the Swift. On pages 106 and 107 is a story written by an Italian astronomer working with the Swift mission that your students may enjoy reading to younger members of their families. It conveys an important point about the Swift mission—that the Swift instrumentation will be able to pinpoint the location of bursts more quickly than ever before to enable instruments to fix on them sooner. In the story, this is compared to the rapid movements of the swift bird in finding and catching its prey.

The Swift Mission

1. Tell students that learning more about the mystery of gamma-ray bursts is the goal of several missions sponsored by the National Aeronautics and Space Administration (NASA), including a mission launched in 2004, called the Swift mission. (Swift is a nationwide and international effort, developed collaboratively in Pennsylvania, Maryland, New Mexico, California, Arizona, Italy, and the United Kingdom.)

2. Explain that Swift has launched a three-telescope space observatory to study gamma-ray bursts. Swift will have the ability to rotate in its orbit so it can point its gamma-ray telescope, its X-ray telescope, and its visible light/ultraviolet telescope at gamma-ray bursts within minutes after the burst first appears! Swift will also scan the sky for new black holes and other possible sources of cosmic gamma-rays. Students and the public will be able to follow the mission and see its findings on the web. (The website for the mission itself is **http://swift.gsfc.nasa.gov** and for the education component is **http://swift.sonoma.edu**).

http://swift.gsfc.nasa.gov
http://swift.sonoma.edu

3. Let students know that, in addition to their scientific work, astronomers working with the Swift mission (and all NASA missions) are very concerned about education. The activities students experienced in this unit are part of this educational effort. Astronomers who work with the Educational and Public Outreach part of the mission helped develop this unit.

Creating a Gamma-Ray Burst Electromagnificent Poster

1. Tell your students that for a special project to end this unit you would like them to design and present a poster on gamma-ray bursts. The poster could represent how powerful gamma-ray bursts are by comparing them to other events, as they did earlier. The poster should also depict some of what they have learned about the electromagnetic spectrum, waves and wavelength, the way humans have made use of the different invisible light rays, and the differing images of objects in space that come from detection in different regions of the spectrum.

Here is a small example of a poster from the "Imagine the Universe!" website at http://imagine.gsfc.nasa.gov/ This is just one example; encourage your students to come up with whatever approaches and designs they think best.

2. Make sure that students know that:
    • the poster does **NOT** have to cover everything!
    • the poster should relate to gamma-ray bursts in some way
    • the poster should be educational and attractive

3. Depending on your students and your assessment needs and preferences, you may want to make the assignment more detailed, giving students a specific checklist or other rubric to explain your criteria to them.

How Much Energy is That?

Event	Energy
Car Crash	ounces of TNT
Large Blast at a Construction Site	30 pounds of TNT
Demolition of 13 Story Hotel in Las Vegas (October 3, 2000)	700 pounds of TNT
Large Quarry or Mine Blast	1 ton of TNT
Small Nuclear Weapon	1,000 tons TNT
Average Tornado	5,100 tons TNT
Atomic bomb (destroyed Hiroshima)	15,000 tons TNT
Formation of Meteor Crater, Arizona	15-20 million tons TNT (Megatons)
Largest Hydrogen Bomb (H-bomb)	32 million tons (32 Megatons)
Earth's Daily Receipt of Solar Energy	50 Megatons of TNT/sec (1.5 H-bombs/sec)

San Francisco Earthquake, 1906 (Magnitude 7.7)	**30 H-bombs (1,000 Megatons TNT)**
Chilean Earthquake, 1960 (Magnitude 9.5)	**1000 H-bombs (32,000 Megatons TNT)**
Creation of Chicxulub Crater, (led to Extinction of Dinosaurs)	**30,000,000 H-bombs (100,000,000 Megatons)**
Total Energy Output of the Sun	**3 billion H-bombs/sec** **300 trillion H-bombs/day** **100,000 trillion H-bombs/yr**
Total Energy Output of a Supernova	**As much as the total output of the Sun (during its 10 billion year lifetime) —in a matter of days!**
Total Energy Output of a Gamma-Ray Burst	**As much as the total energy output of 100 supernovae—in seconds!**

How Much Energy is in a Gamma-Ray Burst? (I)

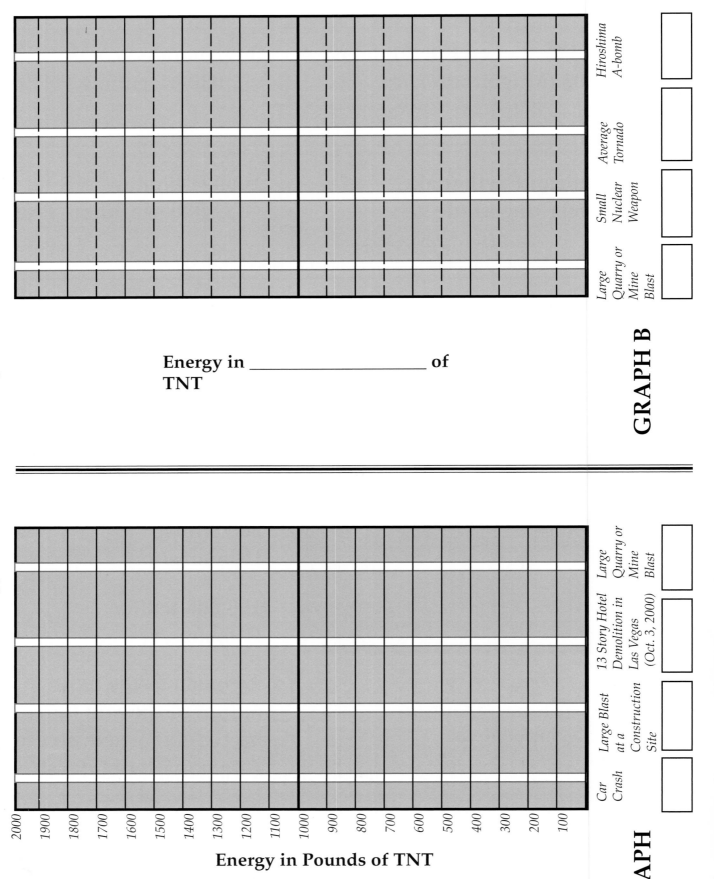

Energy in _____ **of TNT**

GRAPH B

Hiroshima A-bomb

Average Tornado

Small Nuclear Weapon

Large Quarry or Mine Blast

GRAPH A

Large Quarry or Mine Blast

13 Story Hotel Demolition in Las Vegas (Oct. 3, 2000)

Large Blast at a Construction Site

Car Crash

2000 1900 1800 1700 1600 1500 1400 1300 1200 1100 1000 900 800 700 600 500 400 300 200 100

Energy in Pounds of TNT

How Much Energy is in a Gamma-Ray Burst? (II)

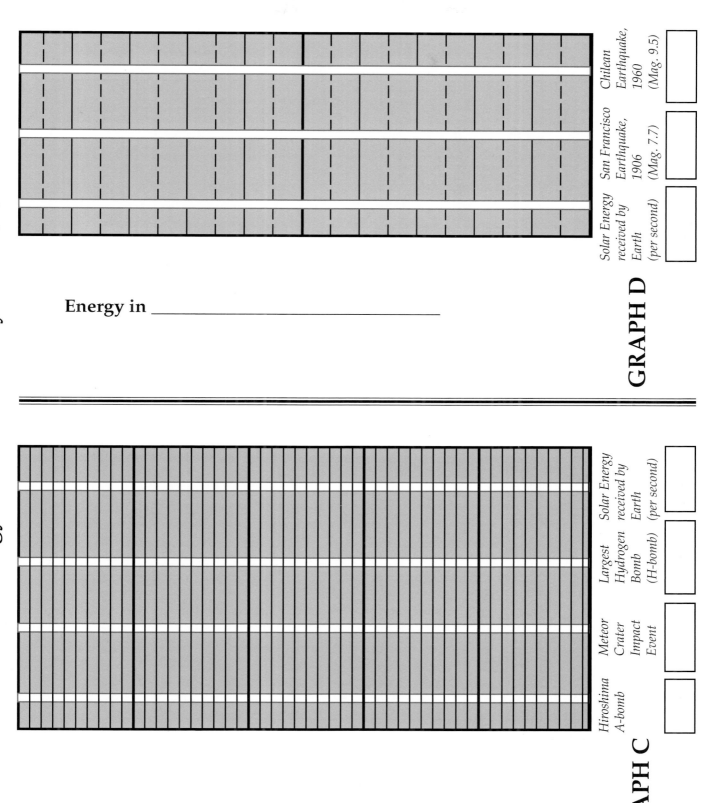

Energy in _____

GRAPH D

- Solar Energy received by Earth *(per second)*
- San Francisco Earthquake, 1906 *(Mag. 7.7)*
- Chilean Earthquake, 1960 *(Mag. 9.5)*

GRAPH C

- Hiroshima A-bomb
- Meteor Crater Impact Event
- Largest Hydrogen Bomb (H-bomb)
- Solar Energy received by Earth *(per second)*

Energy in _____ **of TNT**

How Much Energy is in a Gamma-Ray Burst? (III)

Chicxulub Crater Impact
(dinosaur extinction event)   _____ H-bombs

Total Energy
Output   =   _____ in a sec   H-bombs

_____ in a day   H-bombs

_____ in a year   H-bombs

of the Sun

Total Energy Output
of a Supernova

= _____
   _____
   _____
   _____
   _____

Total Energy Output
of a Gamma-Ray Burst = _____

Meteor Crater and Hiroshima

Barringer Meteor Crater, Arizona
Diameter: 1.186 kilometers (.737 miles)
Age: 49,000 years
Location (near Winslow, AZ): 35° 02'N, 111° 01'W

Photograph of the city of Hiroshima, Japan after the U.S. Army Air Force
dropped the atomic bomb on August 6, 1945.

The Mystery of the Gamma-ray Bursts

In October of 1963 the U.S. Air Force launched the first in a series of satellites to try to detect any violations of a Nuclear Test Ban Treaty that had just been signed. Countries who signed the treaty agreed not to test nuclear devices in the atmosphere or in space. The satellites were designed to monitor the Earth from space to make sure there were no nuclear tests. The satellites were launched and operated in pairs on opposite sides of a circular orbit 250,000 kilometers in diameter (about a 4-day orbit). All parts of the Earth could be observed. The satellites carried X-ray, gamma-ray, and other detectors.

One of the Vela satellites designed to detect nuclear tests that actually detected gamma-ray bursts!

The X-ray detectors were designed to sense the flash of X-rays from a nuclear blast. Although most of the energy of a bomb blast would be sensed as an X-ray flash, the gamma-ray sensors were also needed to confirm that a **nuclear** explosion had taken place.

The gamma-ray detectors would look for gamma-radiation from the cloud of radioactive material that is blown out from a nuclear blast. Even if the explosion happened behind a thick shield (or in a place where the X-ray flash was hidden) the gamma-ray radiation would still be detected. The blast cloud would spread out and be detected by the gamma-ray detectors. Fortunately, in the 1960s and early 1970s, the satellites did not detect a single nuclear explosion— that was very good news!

But something was triggering the gamma-ray detectors. Scientists could tell this was not from nuclear bombs. The data were filed away for future study.

What events could cause these instruments to detect gamma rays? By 1972 scientists had figured out enough about the directions the gamma-rays came from to be sure that neither the Earth nor the Sun were sources. The gamma-ray events were definitely "of cosmic origin," from far out in space. In 1973, this discovery was announced in a scientific paper. The paper discussed 16 cosmic gamma-ray bursts observed between July 1969 and July 1972.

Since then, X-ray and gamma-ray detectors on satellites have confirmed that there are indeed frequent bursts of high-energy radiation coming from space that we can detect. But what are these bursts? Where do they come from?

The mystery of the bursts created lots of excitement among astronomers and other scientists. This led to a "burst" of papers and publications on the newly discovered "gamma-ray bursts." The mystery persists to this day. New missions, like the Swift mission launched in 2004, are planned to investigate many questions: What causes the gamma-ray bursts? How big are these explosions? What can gamma-ray bursts tell us about black holes, about the beginnings and endings of stars and galaxies? What can they tell us about the entire Universe?

The paper referred to was written by Klebesadel, Strong, and Olsen in 1973. This student reading was modified and adapted from *A Brief History of the Discovery of Cosmic Gamma-Ray Bursts* by J.Bonnell, April 17, 1995; http://antwrp.gsfc.nasa.gov/htmltest/jbonnell/www/grbhist.html

Gamma-ray Burst Light Curves

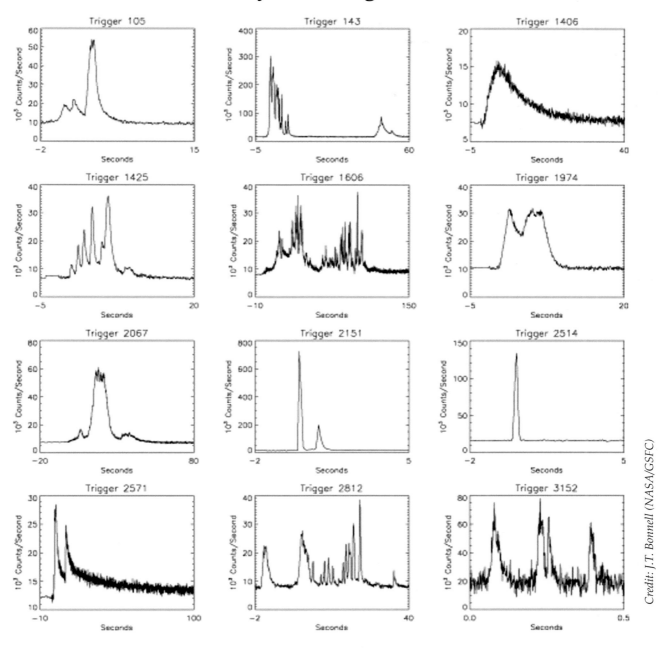

Credit: J.T. Bonnell (NASA/GSFC)

These graphs track data from actual gamma-ray bursts that have been detected by astronomers. They serve as an excellent way to illustrate why these extremely powerful emissions of energy are called "bursts."

(From: http://cossc.gsfc.nasa.gov/images/epo/gallery/grbs index.html)

What You Need for the Whole Unit

Activity 1: Comparing Wave Makers
- ❑ 6 copies of the News Flashes (master on page 24)
- ❑ 32 handouts, *Comparing Wave Makers* (master on page 23)
- ❑ 2 overhead projectors
- ❑ 2 slinkies
- ❑ 2 metal "snaky" springs—about 5-8 meters
- ❑ 2 ropes—thick, heavy, about 5 meters long
- ❑ 2 coiled telephone cords—about 5 meters long
- ❑ 2 flexible rubber or plastic hoses—about 5–8 meters long
- ❑ 1 pitcher for water
- ❑ 2 ripple tanks (flat-bottomed clear plastic tray, dowels, medicine dropper, clear ruler)
- ❑ 1 compass
- ❑ 1 magnet
- ❑ 8 meter sticks

Activity 2: Invisible Light Sources and Detectors
- ❑ 1 overhead transparency of *Invisible Light Sources, Detectors, and Shields* student sheet
- ❑ 1 X-ray film image
- ❑ 6–12 Station Number Signs
- ❑ 6–12 sets of shields/transmitters—one for each station in manila folder or envelope. Each set has: blank overhead transparency, aluminum foil, plain white paper, cloth, metal screen, plastic screen, black plastic, plastic baggie, wax paper
- __ **Station 1**—flashlight with batteries, plain white paper, optional color filters
- __ **Station 2**—infrared bulb with ceramic socket, optional digital or video camera
- __ **Station 3**—remote control with batteries, TV monitor or other device, optional digital or video camera
- __ **Station 4**—FM radio with batteries
- __ **Station 5**—AM radio with batteries
- __ **Station 6**—black light—fluorescent, assortment of: "bright" paper; styrofoam peanuts, detergent, tonic water with quinine in cup, index card with UV paint, glow-in-the-dark stars, UV beads.

Activity 3: Putting Together the Electromagnetic Spectrum
- ❑ 2 sets of the Electromagnetic Spectrum Cards one on card stock and the other as overheads
- ❑ 1videotape player, monitor, and videotape: *The Infrared World: More Than Your Eyes Can See*
- ❑ sources and detectors from Activity 2
- ❑ 1 overhead projector
- ❑ 8 sets of the Electromagnetic Spectrum Cards on card stock (for each group)
- ❑ 32 copies of homework worksheet, *Invisible Emitters and Detectors*

Activity 4: Tour of the Invisible Universe
- ❑ 1 set of the 12 composite overheads for the *Tour of the Invisible Universe*
- ❑ 1 overhead projector or computer projector
- ❑ *Expert's Narration Cards for Tour of the Invisible Universe*
- ❑ 32 *Tour of the Invisible Universe* worksheets (one for each student).

Activity 5: The Most Powerful Explosions in the Universe
- ❑ 1 transparency of *How Much Energy is That?*, of the *How Much Energy is in a Gamma-Ray Burst?* student worksheet, and of the Meteor Crater/Hiroshima images.
- ❑ 1 overhead projector
- ❑ 32 *How Much Energy is in a Gamma-ray Burst?* three-page student worksheets
- ❑ 32 copies of the article *The Mystery of the Gamma-Ray Bursts*

Background for the Teacher

On the Electromagnetic Spectrum

We humans are most familiar with the part of the electromagnetic spectrum that we can see. Our eyes are adapted to see the parts of the electromagnetic spectrum that the Sun emits. In this range, we can perceive different colors with our eyes. A simple experiment with sunlight and a prism shows that sunlight is composed of a range of colors. This same experiment can show that there are other types of light that are beyond the range of the visible.

In an experiment first done by Sir William Herschel, thermometers were placed in and around a spectrum of light from the Sun produced by a glass prism, in an effort to measure the temperature of the colors of the rainbow. Herschel was very surprised to find that the warmest place was in a region just **beyond** the red end of the spectrum. We now call that form of invisible energy *infrared* light (also infrared rays, infrared radiation, infrared waves).

Although infrared and ultraviolet light are the two regions that "bookend" visible light in the electromagnetic spectrum, they only represent two of the regions of invisible light—any light not directly seen by our eyes.

Other creatures have slightly different sensitivities. Many insects can "see" into the ultraviolet region, and various flowers have taken advantage of this sensitivity by having patterns on them that appear most prominently in the ultraviolet. Studies have shown that rattlesnakes (and other pit vipers) have specialized heat-sensing organs in their heads. Pit vipers have pit-like depressions between their nostrils and eyes. These pits are associated with heat-sensitive nerve endings. With these specialized sense organs, the snake can locate its small rodents using the heat given off by their warm bodies. These infrared sensors allow these snakes to hunt at night, and to find warm-blooded rodents whose body temperatures are warmer than ours.

Although humans, unlike snakes, do not have infrared sensing organs, we do have the ability to feel heat with our skin. To sense wavelengths other than visible light we must rely upon detectors of various kinds. These include photographic film and electronic detectors, such as CCD (charge coupled devices) detectors that can be adapted to detect different types of electromagnetic waves. CCD detectors are found in still and video digital cameras and are also used in instruments that detect near-infrared, ultraviolet, and even X-ray wavelengths. These electronic detectors extend the range of our human senses enormously.

In astronomy, specialized electronic detectors coupled to telescopes allow scientists to "see" into the distant Universe. These new detectors have allowed for fantastic views of objects that emit most of their radiation at "invisible" wavelengths.

Visible light is one region of the electromagnetic spectrum. Other electromagnetic regions include radio waves, microwaves, infrared radiation, ultraviolet rays, X-rays, and gamma rays. These forms are known collectively as the electromagnetic spectrum. They are fundamentally similar in that, in a vacuum, they all move at the speed of light: 300,000 kilometers per second (186,000 miles per second). The difference between these regions is that their wavelengths are different. The different wavelengths carry different amounts of energy. The shorter the wavelength, the higher the energy.

When we look at the rainbow of colors in a real rainbow or from a prism, we are looking at only a very small portion of the electromagnetic spectrum—the visible light portion. At one end of the spectrum are radio waves with wavelengths millions to billions of times longer than the visible light we see. At the other end of the spectrum are gamma rays with wavelengths millions to billions of times shorter than the wavelength of visible light. Each part of the electromagnetic spectrum has different useful applications.

Radio Waves

Radio waves, with wavelengths that range from about a meter to tens or even hundreds of meters, transmit the signals for radio and television. (Microwaves are also radio waves, but are in their own category below). Commercial AM radio stations use waves that are about 187 meters to 545 meters in length. An AM station at 750 on the dial (a frequency of 750 kilohertz) uses a wavelength of about 400 meters. Commercial FM radio stations function using shorter radio waves, generally between 2.8 and 3.4 meters in wavelength. For example, an FM radio station at 100 on the radio dial (a frequency of 100 megahertz) would have a wavelength of about 3 meters. Television is carried by waves from 0.4 meters (in the microwave region) to 5.6 meters in wavelength.

Microwave

Microwaves are defined as radio waves between 1 millimeter and one meter in wavelength. In a microwave oven, the radio waves generated are tuned to frequencies that can be absorbed by the food (about 12 centimeters in wavelength). The water in the food absorbs the energy which heats the food. Microwaves are also used by cordless telephones and cell phones. Cell phones generally operate with waves that are either 16 centimeters or 35 centimeters in wavelength.

Infrared

Infrared is the region of the electromagnetic spectrum with wavelengths just longer than the red part of the visible spectrum. The infrared extends from the visible region to where electromagnetic waves are about 1 millimeter in wavelength. Infrared waves include thermal or heat radiation. For example, burning charcoal in an outdoor grill may not give off much light, but the heat from the grill is felt because of the infrared radiation emitted.

Visible Light

The rainbow of colors that we know as visible light is the portion of the electro-magnetic spectrum with wavelengths between 400 (blue) and 700 (red) billionths of a meter (a wavelength of 400 to 700 nanometers. A nanometer is 10^{-9} meters). This is the part of the electromagnetic spectrum that we see, as our eyes are most sensitive in these wavelengths.

Ultraviolet

Ultraviolet light is just outside the blue end of the visible range, being shorter in wavelength than blue light. It is visible to some insects. It has a range of wave-lengths from 400 billionths of a meter to about 10 billionths of a meter. Sunlight contains ultraviolet waves that can burn your skin. Fortunately, most of the harmful ultraviolet wavelengths are blocked by ozone in the Earth's upper atmo-sphere. A small dose of ultraviolet radiation is beneficial to humans, but larger doses cause skin cancer (including melanoma, an often fatal form) and cataracts.

X-rays

X-rays are high-energy waves with very short wavelengths that have great penetrating power and are used extensively in medical applications and in inspecting welds in metals. The Sun gives off X-rays, especially during solar flares and particle eruptions. X-ray images of our Sun can yield important clues to solar flares and can tell us when to watch out for particles from the Sun hitting the Earth and satellites in orbit. X-rays are also given off by very hot (millions of degrees) material in stars and galaxies. The wavelength range for X-rays is from about 10 billionths of a meter to about 10 trillionths of a meter.

For a nice history of X-rays and accessible information about them, see http://www.xray.hmc.psu.edu/rci/contents_1.html

Gamma rays (also see pages 98–99 for more on gamma-ray bursts)

Gamma rays have wavelengths of less than about 10 trillionths of a meter. They are even more penetrating than X-rays. Gamma rays are generated by cosmic objects, radioactive atoms, in nuclear explosions, and are used in many medical applications. Bursts of gamma rays are also seen in space, which could be due to the collapse of a supermassive star, or perhaps the combination or merger of two very dense compact objects such as neutron stars. In each case, the end result is thought to be the birth of a black hole. Images of our Universe taken in gamma rays yield important information on the life and death of stars, and other cataclysmic processes in the Universe.

Cosmic Rays

Cosmic rays are not considered a part of the electromagnetic spectrum, despite their name. Instead of being electromagnetic waves, cosmic rays are high-energy charged particles that travel through space at nearly the speed of light. Their extremely high energies are comparable to those of the most energetic gamma rays. The highest-energy cosmic rays probably come from outside our galaxy and can tell us something about distant objects such as quasars. Cosmic rays are usually detected when they hit the top of the atmosphere, creating massive showers of particles which can give off light. These secondary particles can then be detected by instruments on the ground. Cosmic rays also interact with gas in our galaxy to make gamma rays. A good site to find out more about cosmic rays is at http://helios.gsfc.nasa.gov (The Cosmic and Heliospheric Learning Center).

How are images that we can see (such as those in the "Tour of the Invisible Universe") created from electromagnetic energies that are invisible?

The process begins with detection. As students learn in this unit, all of the regions of the electromagnetic spectrum can be detected, even though only a very small range is visible to the human eye. Depending on whether the detection device is a radio receiver or a gamma-ray detector, the electromagnetic signals, as students have learned, differ in many ways, including wavelength and frequency. But they are all electromagnetic signals, and can be detected as such. The detector can measure the arrival location, time, and energy of the incoming photons. Typically, as energy increases, the source of that energy emits fewer photons. This means that a gamma-ray source emits many less photons than an X-ray source, but those gamma photons are of very high energy. That is why many gamma ray observations, of even the strongest sources, can be weeks in duration—so that the precious few photons can be detected!

Objects that are bright emit more photons than those that are dim. The detectors count how many photons arrive at a certain location in a given time. Scientists then use computer imaging techniques to reconstruct what the emitting object looks like. This process is similar to the way images are constructed of pixels, as on television, a computer screen, on a digital camera—or even at a football game when people hold up many small signs to make a larger image. Colors are assigned to represent different characteristics, such as intensity, temperature, or energy. (See "false color" below.) This process is explained in greater detail, and simulated in a classroom activity described at the *Imagine the Universe!* website:

http://imagine.gsfc.nasa.gov/docs/teachers/lessons/picture/picture_main.html

The GEMS unit Messages from Space: The Solar System and Beyond *opens with an activity in which students receive simulated signals from a radio telescope and decode a binary message. This is similar to the image-making process described on this page. You could consider presenting that unit or a portion of it before teaching* Invisible Universe.

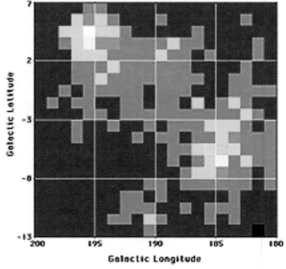

Data After Nine Days

What is meant by "false color"?

The term "false color" is used to describe what astronomers (and others) often do to images to make them more comprehensible. Long ago, when radio astronomers first started generating images of sources, they wound up with essentially images that were just shades of gray—ranging from pure black to pure white. Each shade represented the intensity of the radio emission from a particular part of the object. Radio astronomers took their shades-of-gray images and converted them to color ones by assigning red to the most intense radio emission and blue to the least intense emission recorded on the image. Intermediate colors (orange, yellow, and green) were assigned to the intermediate levels of radio intensity. Black was assigned to places in the image where there appeared to be no radio emission.

This process allows astronomers to more quickly recognize features in the images. Generally, the human eye can only distinguish about 16 shades of gray from one another. Using millions of colors, instead, can often enable scientists to bring out details in an image that might otherwise be missed. At present, just about every area of astronomy creates "false color" images. Remember—electromagnetic radiation does not have "real" color except for the radiation that has a wavelength of between 400 and 700 nm. That little range is called the "visible" spectrum, since it is what we humans beings see with our eyes!

Swift Song Transcript

To hear the song as an MP3 file, go to: http://swift.sonoma.edu/resources/multi/swiftmono.mp3

We know that gamma ray explosions happen randomly all over the sky.
(It's like a lottery: a ticket for each square degree)
You see a FLASH! and then there's not another till about a day has gone by.
(But that depends upon detector sensitivity)
In just a moment they spew energy worth (That's pretty fast)
A value we can't even fathom on Earth, (It's really vast!)
But just what's giving rise to gamma ray sparked skies?
Is it the death cry of a massive star
Or black hole birth? (Or both, or both? or both!)

CHORUS I:
Swiftly swirling, gravity twirling,
neutron stars about to collide,
off in a galaxy so far away,
catastrophic interplay,
a roller coaster gamma ray ride.
Superbright explosion then
never to repeat again
How are we supposed to know?
How about a telescope rotation
swiftly onto the location
of its panchromatic afterglow?

In just a moment gamma ray bursts reach a peak and swiftly fade from view
(It's like a beacon shining clear across the Universe)
But they leave embers in the longer wavelengths fading for a day or two,
(It's exponential—it decays forever)
To solve this space age mystery is why (we wanna know)
We want to catch a thousand bursts on the fly, (what makes 'em go?)

Their X-ray light disperse
Unlock the Universe
Measure their distance from their redshift
Mark their spot on the sky (They're where? They're here!
They're there! They're everywhere!)

Repeat CHORUS I

CHORUS II:
Swiftly swirling, gravity twirling,
neutron stars about to collide,
off in a galaxy so far away,
catastrophic interplay,
a roller coaster gamma ray ride.
Superbright explosion then
never to repeat again
How are we supposed to know?
Swift is the satellite that swings
Onto those brightly bursting things,
To grab the multiwavelength answer of what makes them glow.

It's like a lottery—a ticket for each square degree
It's like a beacon shining clear across the Universe
Swift is the satellite that swiftly swings all over the sky
Swift is designed to catch a burst of gamma rays on the fly.

Gamma-Ray Bursts

What causes gamma-ray bursts? The first burst was detected over 30 years ago and the mystery that surrounds their origin continues to exist. We do know that gamma-ray bursts are the most powerful events to occur in the present-day Universe!

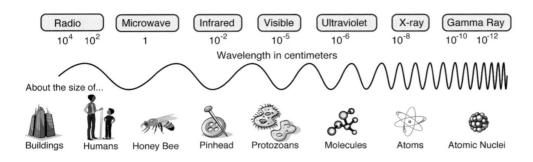

In order to understand what a gamma-ray burst (or GRB) is, students need to recognize gamma-rays as a type of light—the most energetic form of light known.

Light, as a form of electromagnetic radiation, comes in tiny packets of energy called photons with a wide range of energies. At the low-energy end of the spectrum of energies we find radio waves, with a very long wavelength. At the high-energy end of the spectrum we find gamma-rays, with a very short wavelength. The human eye is blind to nearly the entire electromagnetic spectrum, except for the very narrow range of light that falls in the visible range of the spectrum.

If an astronomer were to study the Universe only in the visible range of the spectrum, the large majority of events would go unobserved. Cosmological events such as star birth and star death emit photons with energies across the entire electromagnetic spectrum. Thanks to considerable technological advances, astronomers now have the ability to view the Universe in radio waves, gamma rays, and all energies in between. Pulsars, the fast spinning "cinders" left from supernovae, were first discovered by the radio waves they emit. Galactic dust can be observed in the infrared range, while light from ordinary stars such as the Sun can be observed in the visible and ultraviolet range. Extremely hot gas can be observed by the X-rays that it emits. Observations in the gamma-ray range of the spectrum reveal a very energetic Universe: blazars (which consist of supermassive black holes with jets of particles blasting away from near the event horizon), solar flares, and the radioactive decay of atomic nuclei created in supernova explosions all produce gamma rays.

So what exactly is a gamma-ray burst? At least once a day, the sky lights up with a spectacular flash of gamma rays coming from deep space. The brightness of this flash of gamma rays can temporarily overwhelm all other gamma-ray sources in the Universe. The burst can last from a fraction of a second to over a thousand seconds. The time that the burst occurs and the direction from which it will come cannot be predicted. Currently, the exact cause of these flashes is unknown. Gamma-ray bursts can release more energy in 10 seconds than the Sun will emit in its entire 10 billion-year lifetime. So far, it appears that all of the bursts we have observed have come from outside the Milky Way Galaxy.

The first gamma-ray bursts were detected while scientists were using satellites to look for gamma rays that would result from violations of the Nuclear Test Ban Treaty during the Cold War Era of the 1960s. Gamma rays were found, but the gamma rays were coming from outer space and not from a nuclear bomb exploding in the Earth's atmosphere.

There are several current theories about the possible causes of gamma-ray bursts. One explanation proposes that they are the result of colliding neutron stars—corpses of massive stars (5 to 10 times the mass of our Sun) that have blown up as supernovae. A variation of this theory proposes that gamma-ray bursts are the result of a merging between a neutron star and a black hole or between two black holes. Black holes often result when supermassive (greater than 20 times the mass of our Sun) stars die. A new theory that is attracting considerable attention states that as a result of a hypernova, gamma-ray bursts occur, with material shooting toward Earth at almost the speed of light. A hypernova explosion can occur when the largest of the supermassive stars come to the end of their lives and collapse to form black holes. Hypernova explosions can be at least 100 times more powerful than supernova explosions.

One of the greatest difficulties in finding gamma-ray bursts is that they are so short-lived. Once a burst is detected, it takes too long to reposition the satellite to face the burst and collect data. Recently, scientists were able to observe the visible light from a burst as the burst was occurring. This extraordinary event occurred as the result of a great deal of planning, cooperation, and luck. On January 23, 1999, a network of scientists was notified within 4 seconds of the start of a burst that a burst was in progress. Thanks to the Compton Gamma Ray Observatory, BeppoSAX, the Internet, and a special robotic ground-based telescope, scientists were able to monitor the burst from start to finish at multiple wavelengths. It had the optical brightness of 10 million billion Suns, which was only one-thousandth of its gamma-ray brightness!

The future looks promising for solving the mystery of GRBs. Swift, a satellite with the capacity to study the Universe in a multitude of wavelengths, was launched in November 2004. The satellite is aptly named because once a burst is detected, it can be repositioned to face the gamma ray source within 50 seconds. Observing the burst in the optical (visible light), ultraviolet, X-ray, and gamma-ray ranges of the electromagnetic spectrum, scientists hope to answer the many questions surrounding gamma-ray bursts. In approximately 2006, the Gamma-Ray Large Area Space Telescope (GLAST) will also be launched and should provide scientists with additional insight into the gamma-ray burst mystery.

NASA Gamma-Ray Burst Satellite Team Assembles World's Largest Telescope Mask

March 13, 2002

Greenbelt, MD—The team behind the NASA gamma-ray burst satellite called Swift has completed construction of a massive "coded aperture mask," the largest such device ever built, marking another milestone on its path to its 2004 launch. The mask will be key in pinpointing the location of gamma-ray bursts, the most powerful events in the Universe, whose origins have remained a mystery because the bursts fade within seconds, too quickly to precisely locate and investigate in detail with previous satellites.

The gamma rays that pass through Swift's coded aperture mask will create a shadow upon the gamma-ray detectors below, allowing scientists to trace the location of gamma-ray bursts with great accuracy based on the shape of the shadow. The mask, the size of a standard piece of plywood (4 by 8 feet, or 1.2 by 2.4 meters), comprises approximately 52,000 tiny lead squares spaced in a computer-generated random pattern.

"Each of the 52,000 tiles was hand-placed 'upside down,'" said Danielle Vigneau, the lead engineer for the team that designed and built this coded aperture mask at NASA Goddard Space Flight Center. "We then used a thin coat of wet adhesive to bond all of the tiles to the panel simultaneously as the panel was lowered down on top of the tiles."

Unlike other forms of light, gamma rays penetrate right through focusing mirrors. Thus, this shadowing technique is needed to determine the location of a gamma-ray source. Gamma rays will only pass through the gaps between the lead tiles.

The mask together with a set of gamma-ray detectors, totaling 32,768 pieces of cadmium-zinc-telluride each measuring four square millimeters are the main components of Swift's Burst Alert Telescope (BAT). BAT will locate hundreds of bursts to better than 4-arcminute accuracy and provide enhanced sensitivity to faint bursts that earlier detectors have missed. BAT will relay positions of bursts within 15 seconds to ground-based and other space-based observatories. And during this time, Swift's other two instruments—the X-ray Telescope and Ultraviolet/Optical Telescope—will zoom in upon the BAT detection and provide arcsecond positioning. This will provide for crucial follow-up observations of the burst's lower-energy afterglow, which can last for days to weeks. The data from the BAT will also produce a sensitive hard X-ray (high-energy) all-sky survey about 20 times deeper than previous surveys and uncovering over 400 new supermassive black holes. For this coded aperture mask project, NASA Goddard and Swales Aerospace, Inc., in Beltsville, Md., developed the detailed mask design; Composite Optics, Inc., in San Diego manufactured the honeycomb panel; and the Johns Hopkins University Applied Physics Laboratory in Baltimore manufactured the lead tiles. Mike Schoolman of NASA Goddard is the lead technician for the coded aperture mask.

Swift is a key component of NASA's Structure and Evolution of the Universe theme, which seeks answers to key questions in present-day astrophysics, including what powered the Big Bang, what is the nature of space and time, and what is the Universe made of. Swift was selected in October 2000 as a medium-class explorer mission (MIDEX). Swift, an international collaboration with partners in Italy and Great Britain, will operate for two years or more following launch. Dr. Neil Gehrels from NASA's Goddard Space Flight Center is the Principal Investigator for the Swift Mission. A detailed description of Swift is available at: http://swift.sonoma.edu/ or http://swift.gsfc.nasa.gov

Assembly of the Swift satellite coded aperture mask.

Glossary

Black Hole: The final state of a dead supermassive star, black holes have such strong gravity, that within their event horizons, not even light can escape from their pull.

Comet: Comets are frozen iceballs of dust, gas, and rock. They travel around the Sun in elliptical orbits, with periods ranging from a year or two to tens of thousands of years. Halley's Comet, named for the man who discovered its orbit, Edmund Halley, is perhaps the most famous comet. It returns to the inner Solar System about every 76 years.

Milky Way Galaxy: This is the galaxy within which the Earth and Solar System reside. It is a relatively average spiral galaxy and contains upwards of 200,000,000,000 (2×10^{11}) stars.

Gamma-Ray Photon: As noted in this guide, electromagnetic/light energy is visualized by scientists using both a wave model and a particle model. The particle unit is called a photon. A gamma-ray photon represents the high energy, high frequency, short wavelength end of the electromagnetic spectrum. Like all photons, it moves at the speed of light, 300,000 km/sec (3×10^5 km/sec) and has no mass.

Gamma-Ray Burst: The most powerful explosions known in the Universe today, gamma-ray bursts, or GRBs, "light up" the sky about once a day, but we don't see them with our eyes because they emit almost all of their power in gamma rays. Detected in the late 1960s, and first interpreted in the early 1970s, we are only today making inroads into what causes these mysterious phenomena. GRBs are named using the designation "GRB" and the date of the burst. For example, GRB 990123 was seen to occur in 1999 on January 23 (01/23).

Nebula with Pulsar: After a supernova explosion, the stellar core often collapses into a neutron star, while what used to be the star's outer layers form an expanding shell of gas called a nebula. Sometimes this is referred to as a "supernova remnant." There can be interesting exchanges of energy between the pulsar and the nebula—this is well observed in the Crab Nebula. The Crab supernova took place in 1054 A. D., and was documented by Chinese astronomers.

Optical Photon: represents the medium energy, medium frequency, average wavelength portion of the electromagnetic spectrum—and the part we detect with our eyes! Like all photons, it moves at the speed of light, 300,000 km/sec (3×10^5 km/sec) and has no mass. In the guide, this region of the spectrum is called visible light.

In the early 1900s, during some of the first radiation studies, it was found that heavier atoms can give off three types of radiation: alpha rays, beta rays, and gamma rays. Later it was found that alpha and beta rays were actually pieces of atoms: an alpha ray is a helium nucleus (a combination of two protons and two neutrons) and a beta ray is an electron. Alpha and beta particles can be emitted by a heavy atom at various speeds. However, a gamma ray is electromagnetic, or light energy—photons of electromagnetic radiation. It can only travel at one speed—the speed of light.

Pulsar: A pulsar is a spinning neutron star. It has a mass comparable to an object like our Sun, but is only about 20 km in diameter! That makes for a very dense object, with a large gravitational pull! Neutron stars also have strong magnetic fields—more than 100,000,000,000 (1×10^{11}) times stronger than the magnetic field of the Earth. Pulsars are often named using their coordinates on the sky and the designation "PSR." A typical name might be PSR J1302-6350, where the J represents a standard astronomical coordinate system, and the numbers are the position of the pulsar in those coordinates.

Quasar: Quasars are thought to be caused by a supermassive black hole in the center of an otherwise normal galaxy. They are known to emit enormous amounts of energy. Recent observations imply many have features called jets, which are collimated streams of matter emitted at high velocity from the poles of the quasar. Because light travels at a finite speed, the farther away an object is, the longer it takes for its light to reach us. We see the object as it was when the light left it, which means, as we look farther from the Earth, we are looking into the past! The amount of time in the past that we see an object is called the "lookback time."

Radio Photon: represents the low energy, low frequency, long wavelength end of the electromagnetic spectrum. Like all photons, it moves at the speed of light, 300,000 km/sec (3×10^5 km/sec) and has no rest mass.

For much more on the Sun and its connections to Earth, see the GEMS guides The Real Reasons for Seasons *and* Living with a Star.

Sun: Our nearest star, the Sun gives us the heat and light we need to survive and thrive. Considered an average star, the Sun is about halfway through its estimated 10 billion year main sequence lifetime (burning nuclear fuel in its core to produce the sunlight that we see).

Supernova: When a massive star runs out of fuel, it explodes in a spectacular event called a supernova. New elements are created in the explosions and spewed out into space to form the raw materials of the next generations of stars, planets, and related developments, including the potential for life itself.

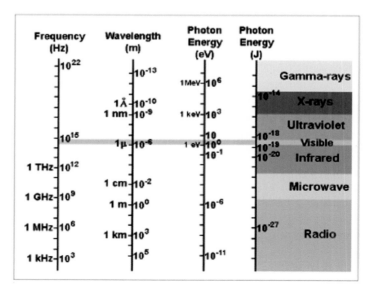

International System of Units (SI)
Metric System Review: Naming Large Numbers

It is difficult to learn about the electromagnetic spectrum without encountering some very large and very small numbers, especially when expressing wavelengths (usually in meters or nanometers) and frequencies (in cycles per second). Scientific notation is very useful for expressing these numbers, as writing a large number of zeroes is tedious and usually a bit confusing.

If your students need more experience with and/or information about large numbers, you may want to have them visit "Ask Dr. Math" online at http://mathforum.org/dr.math/faq/faq.large.numbers.html

Pronunciations of Metric Prefixes

Term	Pronunciation
tera	as in *terra* firma
giga	*gig'* a (i as in *big*)
mega	as in *mega*phone
kilo	*kill'* oh
hecto	*heck'* toe
deka	*deck'* a (a as in *a*-bout)
deci	as in *deci*mal
centi	as in *centi*pede
milli	as in *milli*pede
micro	as in *micro*phone
nano	*nan'oh* (an as in *ant*)
pico	*peek'* o

Multiplication Factor		Prefix	Symbol (Common Name)
1 000 000 000 000 000 000	$= 10^{18}$	exa	E (1 quintillion)
1 000 000 000 000 000	$= 10^{15}$	peta	P (1 quadrillion)
1 000 000 000 000	$= 10^{12}$	tera	T (1 trillion)*
1 000 000 000	$= 10^{9}$	giga	G (1 billion)*
1 000 000	$= 10^{6}$	mega	M (1 million)
1 000	$= 10^{3}$	kilo	k (1 thousand)
100	$= 10^{2}$	hecto	h (1 hundred)
10	$= 10^{1}$	deka	da (ten)
0.1	$= 10^{-1}$	deci	d (one tenth)
0.01	$= 10^{-2}$	centi	c (one hundredth)
0.001	$= 10^{-3}$	milli	m (one thousandth)
0.000 001	$= 10^{-6}$	micro	μ (one millionth)
0.000 000 001	$= 10^{-9}$	nano	n (one billionth)
0.000 000 000 001	$= 10^{-12}$	pico	p (one trillionth)
0.000 000 000 000 001	$= 10^{-15}$	femto	f (one quadrillionth)
0.000 000 000 000 000 001	$= 10^{-18}$	atto	a (one quintillionth)

* Note: Some people recommend that the term billion be avoided, because in most countries outside the U.S. (including the United Kingdom) it means a million-million (prefix tera), but in the U.S. it means a thousand million (prefix giga). Similarly, the term trillion means a million-million-million (prefix exa) in most countries outside the United States.

Units of Energy

Electron-Volt (eV) is an energy unit appropriate for interactions on the scale of one or a few atoms.
Erg (no abbreviation) is appropriate for very delicate processes on a human scale.
Joule (J) is the fundamental energy unit in the "International System of Units," or "S.I.", that is used by scientists. It is a unit appropriate to substantial human-scale processes.
Calorie (cal) is a unit comparable to the joule, but used to measure energy in the form of heat.
Megaton-of-TNT-equivalent (MT) is roughly the explosive energy of a million tons of TNT.
The factors for converting the other units into Joules are:

$1 \text{ eV} = 1.602 \times 10^{-19}$ Joules $1 \text{ erg} = 10^{-7}$ Joules $1 \text{ cal} = 4.186$ Joules $1 \text{ MT} = 4.186 \times 10^{15}$ Joules

Chemical explosives, such as TNT, produce about 1000 joules per gram. There are 453.6 grams in a pound; 2240 pounds in a ton; and 1 million tons in a megaton. The number of joules that a megaton of TNT would produce is: 4.186×10^{15} joules. One ton of TNT would release 4.186×10^{9} joules, and this can be rounded off to: 4.2×10^{9} joules.

Optical light is 2eV.   X-Rays are from 1keV to 100 keV.   Gamma Rays are 1MeV and up.

Astronomical Distances

Astronomers measure the vast distances involved in their work in several ways, including:

Astronomical Unit (AU)—The average distance between the Sun and the Earth. This is about 93 million miles, or 150 million kilometers. It is a good unit to measure distances within a planetary system, such as the Solar System.

Light Year—A unit of length that equals the distance light travels in a year. At the rate of 300,000 kilometers per second (671 million miles per hour), 1 light-year is equivalent to 9.46×10^{12} km, 5,880,000,000,000 miles, or 63,240 AU. Light years are used to describe many of the largest distances in the Universe. "Smaller" distances can be described as light minutes or light seconds. The moon is about 1.5 light seconds from Earth. The Sun is about $8\frac{1}{3}$ light minutes from Earth. Since all electromagnetic signals travel at the speed of light, describing a distance in light years also describes *how long* it would take such a signal to travel that distance. If we sent a radio signal toward the nearest star (other than the Sun), which is about 4.3 light years away, it would take about 4.3 years to get there.

Parsec (pc)—About 3.26 light years

Kiloparsec (kpc) = 1000 parsecs   **Megaparsec (Mpc)** = 1,000,000 parsecs

Parsec is short for parallax second. Parallax is an apparent shift in the position of an object when seen from two different points of view. Careful measurements of parallax shifts can be used to calculate the distance of an object. The distance to some of the closest stars in the Milky Way Galaxy can be found by looking at the stars in the spring, and then again in the fall, when the Earth has traveled halfway around the Sun and is two Astronomical Units from its springtime position. An object that is 1 parsec away will appear to shift one second of arc (1/3600 of a degree) when observed from two places that are two AU apart. Since the measurement of all large distances in space depends on the accurate parallax measurement of close stars, the parsec (or sometimes the megaparsec) has evolved as a measurement for distant objects.

A Few Representative Distances:
The Solar System is about 80 Astronomical Units in diameter.
The nearest star (other than the Sun) is 4.3 light years away.
Our Galaxy (the Milky Way) is about 100,000 light years in diameter.
The diameter of local cluster of galaxies is about 1 Megaparsec.
The distance to M87 in the Virgo cluster is about 50 million light years.

Solar Luminosity

Astronomers measure the Sun's brightness, or solar luminosity, using the metric system. In metric units, 1 solar luminosity equals 400 trillion trillion joules of energy being radiated into space every second. The Earth intercepts only about **one-half billionth** of the energy radiated by the Sun. Yet even this much solar energy gives us sufficient light and warmth.

One Solar Luminosity is comparable to that of four trillion trillion one-hundred-watt light bulbs. If all the energy the Sun radiates in one second could be harnessed, there would be enough energy to satisfy the current U.S. energy usage for about 4 million years!

THE STORY OF A SWIFT AND AN ASTRONOMER

by Monica Sperandio,
English translation By Giuliana Giobbi (edited by L.B.)

Once upon a time...
"...there was a king—my young readers will say" (Collodi, Pinocchio)

No! There was a swift!

Yes, a swift named Anselmo, who had chosen as his nest a nice little cottage with a good solid roof to protect him from the rain, the wind, and the sun, with a beautiful pond nearby—ideal for food. It was indeed the very place for a nest!

So, Anselmo the swift managed to make his nest with a lot of patience, saliva, mud, and blades of grass. Once finished, he looked at it, proud of himself. He had really done a good job! The owner of the cottage was a quiet woman, who gave Anselmo no trouble at all. Sometimes she woke up late in the morning, and she always needed some time to realize she was awake and that a brand new day had just begun! She often wandered around, thoughtful, talking to herself. Aside from this peculiar behavior, the woman seemed harmless. When she went out, she disappeared for a long time, and the swift wondered where the woman went and what she did.

At last, one day, the swift followed her and discovered that the "thoughtful woman"—that's what Anselmo called her— had a really interesting job...she was an ASTRONOMER!

The swift wondered about what he'd found out! He was wondering why that thoughtful woman wanted to gaze at the sky, so far up! After all, she lived in such a beautiful place, with a blue sky filled with a thousand wonders flying above her head every day—butterflies, clouds of many shapes, and—the swift thought—so many tasty insects! Besides, the astronomer had Anselmo too, living just underneath the roof of her cottage, flying over her head every day and every night, even on Sunday, when the thoughtful woman went fishing in the pond! Why on earth was she not satisfied with these wonders? Why did she want to gaze high up in the sky, far above the clouds, where the good swift would never be able to fly?

Our swift got curious and started to follow our astronomer with dangerous flights, through the windows of her study, thus discovering a lot of strange, peculiar details of a world whose existence our bird had never even guessed, a world far above the clouds!! Would you like to find out what is up there, TOO???

Our swift, pushed by his own curiosity, took to accompanying the thoughtful woman to work. She taught ASTRONOMY to groups of young people. The swift tried to get as near as possible to the classroom windows, because he wanted to find out the secrets of the world he could not reach. So he learned a lot about the PLANETS, about the SUN, about our GALAXY, and about other GALAXIES all over the immense UNIVERSE, but he also discovered—and this was both peculiar and extraordinary—that there are also WONDERS THAT CANNOT BE SEEN BY THE HUMAN EYE.

So Anselmo the swift finally realized what made the astronomer so thoughtful.

The astronomer had of course noticed the presence of the swift that followed her everywhere. Even though she liked it, she was not easily distracted from her thoughts. The problem was that astronomers had discovered strange, never-before-known events taking place in the sky. It was a sort of FIREWORKS! Yes, violent explosions were taking place here and there within the universe. That was the problem—HERE and THERE! No one could foresee where an explosion would take place next! So how could they study it? You did not know where to look, and the explosions were so sudden! How could you discover their cause? What happened after this sort of fireworks?

One day, the astronomer got back home earlier than usual. The swift realized at once that his friend looked tired. The poor swift would have liked to help his friend, but what could he do? The swift observed the astronomer's movements very carefully. She let herself in, and went out again almost immediately with her fishing pole. She walked toward the pond and sat down in the shadow of a tree near the shore. While waiting for a fish to take the bait, she thoughtfully looked at the sky—not the sky she normally watched through her telescope—but the sky underneath the clouds. She realized that, in that part of the sky, her faithful swift was performing incredible acrobatics to catch the insects flying over the pond surface. Oops! The bird caught a mosquito in flight, and at the same time saw a beetle and—was off to the other end of the pond! The swift changed his direction all of a sudden, with amazing accuracy and speed. He pounced upon that tasty insect on a grazing flight. While watching the swift's acrobatics, the speed at which he changed direction and exactly how he caught his prey, our astronomer suddenly felt very happy!

Here was the solution to her problem, just in the wonderful sky above her own head! Now she knew what she had to do with her team of scientists. They would build a wonderful spaceship that, just like the swift catching the mosquito, would readily and quickly catch the events animating deep space, with space flights and acrobatics just like her faithful bird!

In the following days, the swift realized that the woman had a different look, shall we say...less thoughtful, almost satisfied. She went out at a jogging pace and came back late, but with a self-confident air, despite how tired she was.

Finally, one day, peeping into the window of the astronomer's study, the swift discovered something that made him very proud: the astronomer and her COLLEAGUES had planned a wonderful machine inspired by Anselmo's own acrobatics, and they called it SWIFT, so the whole world would think of him. The spaceship named in his honor would fly way up above, to places where Anselmo could not fly, to discover unseen wonders of the Universe.

Assessment Suggestions

Selected Student Outcomes

1. Students are able to investigate and draw conclusions about wave motion, including a basic understanding of the inverse relationship between wavelength and frequency.

2. Students demonstrate their understanding of the distinction between sources (and reflectors) of light/energy; transmitters of light/energy; and detectors of light/energy.

3. Students increase their understanding and knowledge of the electromagnetic spectrum, including its main regions (radio, microwave, infrared, visible, ultraviolet, X-ray, gamma ray) and their distinguishing characteristics, attributes, and uses. Students understand that there is a wide range of electromagnetic energy in addition to the light we see, and we can detect these invisible energies with various types of sensors/detectors, including detectors on satellites in space.

4. Students gain increased insight into and understanding of the ways that invisible regions of the electromagnetic spectrum have been instrumental in modern astronomy and have enabled astronomers to gain information about objects and events millions and even billions of light years away from Earth.

5. Students are able to explain how gamma-ray bursts were first detected, to describe and compare their power to other events, and to demonstrate awareness that the cause of gamma-ray bursts is still being investigated.

Embedded Assessment Opportunities

Wave Motion. In Activity 1, which focuses on wave motion, teachers can observe student groups working with the various wave makers, and teacher review of student worksheets will be helpful in gauging how well students have understood the basic objectives of the activity. (Outcome 1)

Detecting Invisible Energy Sources. In Activity 2, teacher observation of student groups and review of the student data sheets should provide good information on student understanding of sources, detectors, transmitters, and shields. Student participation in classroom discussions during the activity will also provide a general sense of initial student understanding. (Outcome 2)

Sorting and Synthesizing. Student sorts of the Electromagnetic Spectrum Cards in Activity 3 will provide insight into student creativity and ability to carefully analyze descriptive scientific information. Classroom discussion of issues such as the relationship of wave cycle length to energy and the nature of infrared vision can help demonstrate how well students are synthesizing and making inferences from what they've learned so far in the unit. (Outcomes 2, 3)

Taking the Tour. Teacher observations of student participation during the tour and of their worksheets will provide some indication of student awareness of distance and location of objects in the Universe, as well as help gauge student skills of observation and description. (Outcome 4)

The Power of Gamma-Ray Bursts. In Activity 5, students make a series of graphs to compare different explosive/energetic events and help them comprehend the power of gamma-ray bursts. Teacher review of student work can provide insight into students' mathematical understanding of large numbers and graphing abilities. (Outcome 5)

Electro-Magnificent Poster. At the end of Activity 5, students are asked to create a poster to represent the power of gamma-ray bursts. Students are also asked to apply the knowledge they have gained during the unit to the poster. Depending on the criteria established by the teacher, this assignment could provide an excellent assessment of student learning. (Outcomes 1–5)

Additional Assessment Ideas

Writing On Invisible Waves. Following Activity 3, or at the end of the unit, students could be given a writing assignment to explain to a student of their own age who has not taken the class what "invisible waves" are and how they can be detected and used.

Pop Quizzes. Design some multiple-choice, true-false, or other brief questions on the content of each activity. (See marginal note.)

Theorizing. At the completion of the unit, students could write and illustrate their own explanation or theory of what could be causing gamma-ray bursts.

Researching the Spectrum. The stories of how the non-visible regions of the electromagnetic spectrum were first detected by scientists are fascinating and, in some cases, also demonstrate dangers to human health. Students could research this history, focusing on one or more regions.

Dramatizing the Spectrum. A group of students could plan and present a dramatization of the electromagnetic spectrum. If they like the "rap" that appears in the back of this GEMS guide, they could use that, or they could come up with their own interpretations. Each student could represent one of the main regions on the spectrum— how are they alike? How are they different? After the presentation the class could ask questions of each character.

The NASA Swift Mission. Launched in November 2004; students could keep track of the mission and report on its progress and findings.

For Activity 1, a quiz question could be: Which statement below best expresses the relationship between wavelength and frequency?
a. There's no known relationship between them.
b. As frequency increases, wavelength decreases.
c. As frequency increases, wavelength also increases.
d. Wavelength is the square root minus one of frequency.

Or, for Activity 4, students could be asked to categorize a list of space objects, using S for inside the Solar System, G for outside the Solar System but inside the Milky Way Galaxy, and O for outside the Milky Way Galaxy.

Resources

Bending Light: Dozens of Activities for Hands-on Learning
by Pat Murphy with Paul Doherty, Jenefer Merrill, and Exploratorium staff;
illustrated by Denise Brunkus
Little, Brown, Boston, MA   (1992; 48 pp.)
> Simple experiments introduce the basic principles of light and lenses.

Cosmic Mysteries
by the editors of Time-Life Books
Time-Life Books, Alexandria, VA   (1990; 144 pp.)
> As part of the Voyage Through the Universe series, this book includes such topics as gamma ray bursts, formation of stars, and astrophysics.

Flash! The hunt for the biggest explosions in the universe
by Govert Schilling
Cambridge University Press, Cambridge, United Kingdom (2002; 291 pp.)
> Excellent scientific journalism for adults and older students by a Dutch science writer telling the story of gamma-ray bursts, with interviews and detailed information on past, current, and future missions, including Swift.

How Did We Find Out About Microwaves?
by Isaac Asimov; illustrated by Erika Kors
Walker, New York, NY   (1989; 63 pp.)
> Describes the discovery of microwaves and explains how they function and their many uses.

How Did We Find Out About Solar Power?
by Isaac Asimov; illustrated by David Wool
Walker, New York, NY   (1981; 62 pp.)
> Describes the uses of the Sun's energy from the time of the Greeks and Romans to the present day and discusses the potential of this source of energy in our modern world.

The Invisible World of the Infrared
by Jack R. White
Dodd, Mead, New York, NY   (1984; 124 pp.)
> Discusses what infrared is; how it is used in science, in space, in the military, and in lasers today; and its incredible possibilities in the future.

The King's Chessboard
by David Birch; illustrated by Devis Grebu
Dial Books, New York, NY   (1988; 32 pp.)
> A proud king learns a valuable (and exponential) lesson when he grants his wise man a request for rice that doubles with each day and square on the chessboard. This tale involves exponential growth.

Light
by David Burnie
Dorling Kindersley, New York, NY   (1992; 64 pp.)
> An Eyewitness Science guide to the origins, principles, and historical study of light.

The Mysterious Rays of Dr. Röntgen
by Beverly Gherman; illustrated by Stephen Marchesi
Atheneum, New York, NY   (1994; 24 pp.)
> Describes the work of Wilhelm Röntgen, the German physicist who
> won the first Nobel Prize in Physics in 1901 for his discovery of X-rays.

Out of Sight: Pictures of Hidden Worlds
by Seymour Simon
SeaStar Books, New York, NY   (2000; 48 pp.)
> Shows pictures of objects which are too small, too far away, or too fast
> to see without mechanical assistance such as microscopes, telescopes, X-
> rays, and other techniques.

Signals from Outer Space: The Chandra X-Ray Observatory
by Robert Naaeye
Raintree Steck-Vaughn Publishers, Austin, TX   (2000; 64 pp.)
> This book is designed for middle-school students. The author has also written
> a prize-winning article in *California Wild* magazine, entitled "Superman's Tele
> scope: The Achievements of Chandra," which is on-line at:
> www.calacademy.org/calwild/summer2001/stories/chandra2sl.html

Waves: The Electromagnetic Universe
by Gloria Skurzynski
National Geographic Society, Washington, DC   (1996; 48 pp.)
> Examines different kinds of electromagnetic waves—including radio
> waves, microwaves, light, X-rays, and gamma rays.

What Do You See & How Do You See It? Exploring Light, Color, and Vision
by Patricia Lauber; photographs by Leonard Lessin
Crown, New York, NY   (1994; 48 pp.)

Internet Sites
In addition to the many sites mentioned throughout the guide, especially
the wide range of NASA-related sites (starting at www.nasa.gov), as well as
NASA for Kids (www.nasa.gov/kids.html),The Space Place
(www.spaceplace.nasa.gov), and the Swift Mission education site
(http://swift.sonoma.edu), several other useful sites include:

Astronomical Society of the Pacific—www.astrosociety.org/education.html
This organization offers many educational resources and helpful web links.

Goddard Space Flight Center—http://imagers.gsfc.nasa.gov/ems/ems.html
A thorough description of the electromagnetic spectrum and a tour of each wavelength. On the visible light page is a good description of true and false colors.

Space Foundation—www.spacefoundation.org
An international organization that has worked with over 12,000 teachers since 1986
through its Teaching With Space, Space Discovery, and Space in the Classroom K–12
professional development programs.

SETI Institute—www.seti.org
Excellent site for update on recent astronomical issues relating to the possibility of life
elsewhere in the Universe, as well as many educational programs and publications.

X-ray History—www.xray.hmc.psu.edu/rci/
This Pennsylvania State University website includes a fascinating pictorial survey of
the discovery and early usage of X-rays, with information and images from Radiology
Centennial, Inc.

Summary Outlines

Activity 1: Comparing Wave Makers

Gamma-Ray Burst Mystery
1. Ask six students to read the news flashes. Discuss the mystery.
2. Say astronomers now detect gamma-ray bursts about once a day!
3. To find out more, students will investigate waves of invisible energy.

Demonstrating Waves
1. Stress that a wave model is one way scientists visualize the movement of energy.
2. Demonstrate wave motion with a student volunteer. Demonstrate standing waves.
3. Ask student volunteers to see how many wave cycles can fit on the spring.

Terms and Relationships
1. Define wavelength, frequency, amplitude.
2. Ask questions to help class respond: What's the relationship between wavelength and frequency? Is amplitude related to wavelength or frequency? Which takes more energy to produce: waves of high frequency, shorter wavelength *OR* of low frequency, longer wavelength?
3. Ask "In what other materials can you produce waves?"
4. Point out that waves can be viewed as a flow of information rather than of material or mass.
5. Demonstrate how to operate the ripple tank. Have students circulate to wave making stations.

Reporting Wave Findings
1. Have groups report their findings.
2. Remind students that frequency is a measure of how many waves go by per second.

Waves Made of Invisible Forces
1. Tell class light waves have frequency of a hundred million million (10^{14}) times per second! How fast does light travel? [300,000 km/sec or 186,000 mi/sec]
2. Ask what light waves are made of. Explain that they are made of electric and magnetic fields—waves of invisible force. Ask, "Can you think of any other invisible forces?" [Gravity, magnetism]
3. Demonstrate "action-at-a-distance" with compass and magnet.
4. Light waves are electromagnetic waves. Gamma rays are also, with extremely high frequencies and very short wavelengths.

Activity 2: Invisible Light Sources and Detectors

Introducing the Activity
1. Shine flashlight at the students. Say, "This flashlight is a source of light."
2. Ask, "What are some other sources of light energy that we can see?"
3. Explain that, while most objects reflect light to some extent, they are not the source.

Detectors, Transmitters and Shields
1. Ask where light detectors are in the room?" [eyes]
2. Ask for other light detectors?" [Cameras, camcorders...]
3. Materials that let visible light through are called transmitters.
4. Some materials do not let light through; they block it, are shields.
5. Using the "Visible Light" station, show how light can be blocked.
6. Ask about other things that block visible light?" [black plastic, paper]
7. Ask, "What are some things that don't shield light, but transmit light, that let light through?" [glass, clear plastic, water, oil] Demonstrate.

Station Introduction
1. In addition to visible light energy in the room, there's invisible energy.
2. Stations are set up with a source of energy, a detector, and a set of materials as test shields.
3. There are six stations. They will work in groups; each student will keep a record of observations on "Sources and Detectors" sheets.

Demonstrate Station Procedure
1. Model the process, again using Station 1.
2. Identify the source (flashlight), the "detector" (white paper), and the set of test shields. (Note that white paper is actually a reflector)
3. Use overhead of worksheet to show how to record predictions and results.

Identifying Sources and Detectors
1. Identify Source and Detector at each station.
2. Discuss any issues that arise, such as the source of radio waves.

Student Groups Experiment at Stations
1. Divide class into groups. Give set of shields/transmitters to each group.
2. Tell students they will have about 7–10 minutes per station.
3. At each switch, remind students to make predictions.
4. Circulate among the groups as needed.

Discussing Invisible Light Findings
1. Have each group report their results from the last station they worked on.
2. For each station, ask questions. Encourage other groups to ask questions.
3. As students respond, summarize on a chart or overhead.
4. To familiarize students with invisible light region, ask questions such as: "What is the name of the light on the remote control?" [infrared], and so on.
5. Ask, "What kind of invisible energy do we cook with?" [microwaves] "What kind of waves are received/transmitted by satellite TV dish?" [microwaves]
6. Hold up or project X-ray image, and discuss dental X-rays and shields.
7. Say that even though people can't see invisible waves, some animals can.
8. Remind students unit began with news flashes on gamma-ray bursts.

Activity 3: Putting the Electromagnetic Spectrum Together

The Elephant and the Spectrum
1. Read elephant poem out loud (or students read it) and discuss its meaning.
2. The search for information about the Universe could be compared to the parable.
3. Have students recall some of the electromagnetic waves they investigated. Ask which animals are sensitive to infrared and ultraviolet waves.
4. Elicit and discuss the main parts/regions of the electromagnetic spectrum.
5. Divide the class into groups.

Sorting and Classifying
1. Tell students each group will have 10 cards and 10-15 minutes to sort the cards in any way they choose. Emphasize there is no one "right`" way.
2. Distribute cards. Circulate among the groups.
3. When finished, reconvene class and ask each group to report on the way(s) they sorted, with full discussion.

Sorting By Wavelength or Energy
1. Acknowledge all their sorts. Tell class a common scientific way is to arrange the cards in order by wavelength, starting with the longest, radio waves.
2. Have volunteers display a full set of cards in this order, with radio waves on the left, on the wall or other place visible to the class.
3. Ask, "Did you notice a connection between the length of a wave cycle and the amount of energy?" Encourage discussion so students understand it is inverse relationship. What region has most energy? [gamma rays] Least? [radio waves].
4. Summarize by telling students that this arrangement is called the electromagnetic spectrum. All of the waves are electromagnetic energy.

Astronomical Observations
1. Explain that one important use for knowledge of the spectrum is in astronomy.
2. Some electromagnetic waves emitted by objects in space make it through the atmosphere, while other wavelengths are blocked (absorbed) by the atmosphere.
3. Ask students to use their cards to respond to the question: "Which wavelengths are absorbed by the atmosphere?"
4. If you were able to display the sources/emitters from Activity 2, ask a group to match their cards with them.

The World of Infrared
1. Ask, "What would the world look like with infrared eyes?"
2. Have students write down predictions.
3. Allow about five minutes writing time, then show the video and discuss.
4. Like infrared, all regions of the spectrum can provide information.
5. As homework, have students list objects that emit or detect invisible light.

Activity 4: Tour of the Invisible Universe

Introducing the Tour
1. Students will take a tour of the Universe to see what various things look like through the "eyes" of detectors that astronomers use.
2. Astronomers began using X-rays. They are now using detectors for all wavelengths.
3. Ask students to name some astronomical objects. Jot down some.
4. Using the list, ask which of the objects are: inside our Solar System; outside our Solar System but inside our galaxy; outside our galaxy.

Taking the Tour of the Universe
1. During the tour, read, or have students read the Expert's Narration.
2. Have students write down observations and compare images.
3. Students record whether object is in Solar System, galaxy, or farther.
4. Begin the tour. Encourage participation with questions.

After the Tour
1. Ask for reactions. What did they like most? Did anything surprise them?
2. Let students know that these are just a few examples from many images.
3. Placing instruments in space has allowed people to "see" the Universe as never before.
4. Remind students that several of the images are related to gamma-ray bursts.

Activity 5: The Most Powerful Explosions in the Universe

Back to the Mystery
1. Remind students of the "News Flashes," that gamma-ray bursts are the most powerful energy explosions in the Universe and are detected about once a day.
2. Hand out article on gamma-ray bursts and have students read it, taking notes, and writing down questions they have. Discuss.
3. Tell students that the power is so massive it is very hard to grasp. One way is to compare it to other powerful events. To do this, they'll make a series of graphs.

Graphing Powerful Events
1. Distribute graphing worksheets to each student.
2. Project the first page of "How Much Energy is That?" Cover the right side.
3. Have students "guesstimate" what the amount of energy would be for the first event (car crash), then reveal it. Do the same for the next.
4. Now focus student attention on the graphing sheets.
5. Proceed through Graphs A, B, C, and D as described in the guide.
6. If students did not switch to the "H-bombs" unit in Graph D, they need to do so. At supernova, the unit needs to change to "the total output of the Sun during its entire lifetime." Then the power of gamma-ray bursts can be expressed in number of supernovae.
7. Point out the short periods of time over which energy is released. Gamma-ray bursts last only minutes, and sometimes seconds!
8. Ask, "What might be causing such incredibly powerful events?"

The Swift Mission/Poster
1. Tell students that learning more about the mystery of gamma-ray bursts is the goal of several NASA missions, including the Swift mission.
2. Swift has launched a three-telescope space observatory to study gamma-ray bursts (http://swift.sonoma.edu)
3. Say that Swift astronomers (and all NASA missions) are very concerned about education. The activities in this unit are part of the NASA educational effort.
4. Tell students that for a special project to end this unit you would like them to design and present a poster on gamma-ray bursts.

Rap of the Electromagnetic Spectrum

Let me first snap my fingers and give you a wave
'Cause wave upon wave is all that I crave
I'm pulsing with energy, glowing with light
A bit you can see, but the rest's outta sight

    From a microwave oven to X-ray machine (involve class)
    Energy's all around you, seen and unseen

Electromagnetic spectrum, that's me
Discover my parts to solve this mystery
I'm actually one big energy action,
But people find in me many attractions

    From a microwave oven to X-ray machine   (with class)
    Energy's all around you, seen and unseen

All of my energy's one and the same
But people have given my waves different names
Like, all of you's you, as everyone knows
But each part's got a name, from your nose to your toes
I've got all kinds of rays, like gamma and X
And each kind of ray has its special effects

    From a microwave oven to X-ray machine (with class)
    Energy's all around you, seen and unseen

Let me put it directly, imagine that you
Were relaxin' at home, the school day was through
Would you read by a light or watch some TV
Dance to a CD, use electricity?
Maybe that night you'd gaze at the stars
Pick up a telescope, see Venus or Mars
Did you know that astronomers also can "see"
On the other wavelengths of my energy?

    From a microwave oven to X-ray machine (with class)
    Energy's all around you, seen and unseen

See, whatever you'd do, however you'd do it
The electromagnetic spectrum runs through it
It's far past the rainbow, spreads far and wide
Light we see's in the middle but there's more on each side!
From a radio wave to a strong gamma ray
The spectrum (that's me) is a part of your day
So pick up your fingers and give 'em a snap
That is the electromagnetic rap!

by L.B.

Another Take on the Elephant

(Modified by L.B. from the poem by John Godfrey Saxe that appears on page 41)

Six women of science in Indostan
To learning much inclined,
Went to see the Elephant
To see what they could find,
So each by observation
Could satisfy her mind.

The first approached the Elephant
And, happening to fall
Against his broad and sturdy side,
At once began to call:
"Sisters, here the Elephant
Feels something like a wall!"

The second woman felt the tusk,
Cried, "Ho! what have we here
Cylindrical and smooth and sharp?
To me 'tis very clear
This portion of an Elephant
Is very like a spear!"

The third approached the animal
And, happening to take
The squirming trunk within her hands,
Thus boldly up she spake:
"I see," quoth she, "this part indeed
Elongates like a snake!"

Another reached an eager hand,
To probe about the knee:
"This part of this most wondrous beast
Is mighty plain," quoth she;
"'Tis clear enough this solid part
Seems something like a tree!"

The next assayed to touch the ear,
Said, "This is quite a span
I think what this resembles most;
Deny it if you can:
This flapping part of Elephant
Is shaped quite like a fan!"

Still, their science was not done
The next did more than grope
She seized upon the swinging tail
That fell within her scope,
"I say," quoth she, "this hanging thing
Is rather like a rope!"

And then the women of science
Considered carefully,
Put all their data together
Scientifically
To well describe the Elephant
In its entirety!

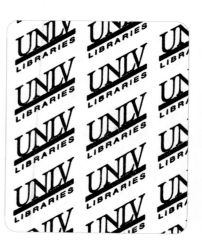

116

People in my family

Bobbie Kalman

The In My World Series

The In My World Series
Conceived and coordinated by Bobbie Kalman

Writing team:
Bobbie Kalman
Maria Protz
Diane Cook-Brissenden
Susan Hughes

Editors:
Susan Hughes
Lise Gunby
Ruth Chernia

Cover and title page design:
Oksana Ruczenczyn, Leslie Smart and Associates

Design and mechanicals:
Ruth Chernia

Illustrations:
Title page by Karen Harrison © Crabtree Publishing Company 1985
Pages 28-32 by Deborah Drew-Brook-Cormack
© Crabtree Publishing Company 1985
Pages 4-27 and cover © Mitchell Beazley Publishers 1982

Cataloging in Publication Data

Kalman, Bobbie, 1947–
    People in my family

(The In my world series)
ISBN 0-86505-061-9

1. Family – Juvenile literature. I. Title.
II. Series.

HQ734.K34 1985   j306.8′5

To Vhari Jean

350 Fifth Avenue
Suite 3308
New York, N.Y. 10118

102 Torbrick Avenue
Toronto, Ontario
Canada M4J 4Z5

Contents

Families grow in different ways

My name is Maggie.
My mommy is going to have a baby.
No one knows what our baby will be like.
Each baby is like a surprise package.
Each baby is different.

In three more months, I'll have a
new baby brother or sister.
It takes nine months for the baby
to grow in Mommy's uterus.
Our baby has been growing for six months.
That's why Mommy's tummy looks so big!
I have a big tummy too,
but not as big as Mommy's.

I was born six years ago.
My mommy didn't go to the
hospital to give birth to me.
She and Daddy adopted me.
They had to wait three years.
Three years is a long time to wait.
Mommy says it was worth it,
because I'm special.
Soon another special person will be
coming into our family.
I can hardly wait to be a big sister!

Picture talk

Why are these women at the doctor's office?
What is the little boy listening to?
Maggie came into her family in a
different way than the new baby will.
What does "adopted" mean?
How do you know Maggie is happy
about the new baby?

4

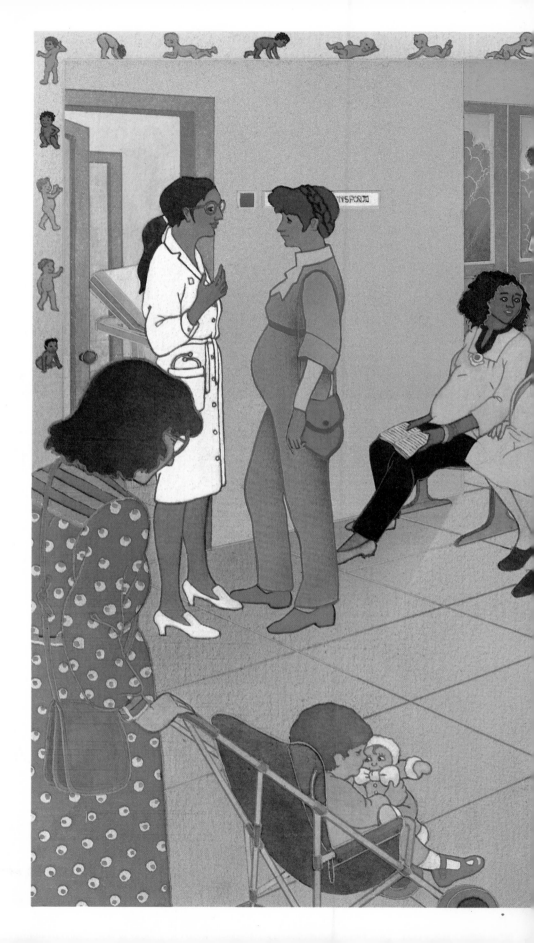

My brother and I are twins

Eduardo and I are twin brothers.
We were born on the same day.
We look alike, but we're different in many ways.
Eduardo is better than I am at arithmetic.
I am better than he is at reading.
Eduardo likes to talk, and I like to listen.

I share all my secrets with Eduardo.
We play catch and tag together.
We share our jobs too.
I love Eduardo, but sometimes I get
tired of looking so much like him.
Mom and Dad can tell us apart,
but not many other people can.
Sometimes I am blamed for
something Eduardo did wrong.
That makes me angry.
I say, "I'm Ernesto, not Eduardo."

Looking alike is usually fun.
Sometimes Eduardo and I fool people.
Last week, we changed clothes at recess.
The teacher wasn't sure who was who.

Mrs. Martinez, the grocer, always blinks
a lot when she sees us.
She pretends she's seeing double.
We all laugh about it.

Picture talk

What job are Ernesto and Eduardo doing?
Is this job more fun to do with a twin?
Would you like to be a twin? Why?
What would be the best part about being a twin?

My mom and I

My name is Ingrid.
My mother is a potter.
Mom's workshop and store are on
the first floor of our house.
The two of us live on the second floor.

Mom teaches people how to make pots.
Her students learn to shape the
clay on the potter's wheel.
They bake their pots in a special oven
called a kiln.
Then the students paint the baked pots.

I want to learn to make pots too.
Mom is teaching me.
I am still too small to use the potter's wheel.
Instead, I roll long clay snakes
and coil them into pots or plates.

My mom is a very good potter.
Many people buy her pots and dishes.
Customers come to her shop, and
choose the pots they like the best.
Mom travels to craft fairs and art shows
so that more people can see her work.
Sometimes she takes me with her.
Sometimes a babysitter takes care of me
while Mom is away.

Picture talk

Where are the potter's wheels and the oven?
Have you ever made anything with clay?
How did the clay feel in your hands?
What things does your mother make
with her hands?

I miss my dad

Boy, was I mad when my dad moved out!
I told him I didn't want to see him again.

Last week my mother told my brother and
me that we were going to visit my dad.
"Your daddy loves you very much, Alicia,
even though we don't live together anymore,"
my mother said.
"Well, I don't care," I answered.
"I don't want to see Dad!"
The funny thing was—I missed Dad a lot.

My brother Victor couldn't wait to see Dad.
When we arrived at my dad's house
for the weekend, Daddy told Victor that
he had built a go-cart just for us.

When I saw my dad, I felt happy inside.
I still acted mad on the outside.
Daddy showed me the go-cart.
He said he would teach me how to drive it.
I told him I wanted to drive it myself.
Then I crashed the go-cart into the wall!
I hurt my knee and cried.
Victor brought me a bandage.
Daddy washed my knee.

It felt good to be sitting on my dad's knee.
I cried for a long time.
Daddy told me it was okay to cry.
My knee didn't hurt anymore.
I cried because I was happy to be
with Daddy again.

When Mom is away

The supper Dad cooked was delicious.
He made spaghetti, and we had
chocolate ice cream for dessert.
When we finish the dishes tonight,
we're going to a movie.

My mother writes stories for a magazine.
She often has to travel.
She is away in another city now.
I miss Mom when she goes away,
but I know she'll be back soon.
Sometimes she calls us
long distance to say hello.
I know she misses us when she's gone.

Dad thinks of fun things for us to do.
Today we built a snowman
which looks just like him.
We also painted a Welcome Back sign
to surprise Mom when she comes home.

Tonight Dad will try to sing us to sleep.
He always does.
We always end up laughing.
He's much better at scratching backs
than singing.

Picture talk

Who does the cooking at your home?
What jobs do your parents share?
How would you feel if you did not see
your parents every day? Why?
How is this family sharing the
after-dinner cleanup?

My grandparents live with us

Two sets of parents live in my house.
My parents and my mother's parents live here.
My mother's parents are my grandparents.
I call my grandma Oma.
I call my grandpa Opa.

My mother and father both work,
so my grandparents look after us.
I think they're terrific.
They know the answers to most of my questions.

My grandparents are good at games.
Opa loves to play cards by himself.
When I come home from school,
he sets them aside.
We play Snakes and Ladders.
Snakes and Ladders is my favorite game.
I have to slide my yellow chip
down a snake for my move.
My friend Olga's blue chip is ahead.
She is winning.

Rudy is playing checkers with Oma.
Oma usually lets him win, but not this time.
Little Hans is playing with dominos.
He likes us to watch while he builds with them.
Then he knocks them over.

Picture talk

How many grandparents do you have?
Do any uncles, aunts, or cousins live with you?
What do you like to do with your grandparents?
Is your favorite game in the picture?

Our papa works at home

Here comes my mother!
She is waving at us through the rain.
I bet she can't wait to get inside
with us where it's dry.
When she comes in, we'll give her
something hot to drink.

Momma is a real-estate agent.
She helps people to buy and sell houses.
She works very hard and comes home late.
Momma wishes she had more time with us.

Papa is the manager of our apartment building.
This means he rents out the apartments.
He calls the plumber or the
electrician when there is a problem
with the pipes or the lights.

I am glad that Papa is the manager
of our building.
This means he takes care of us
when we come home from school.
We do fun things together.
After we tidy the house, we draw
pictures or build towers from blocks.
I like it best when Papa tells us stories
about himself when he was a boy.

Picture talk

Where do your parents work?
When do they work?
How do your parents take turns caring for you?
Who else looks after you?
What family games do you play when
it is raining outside?

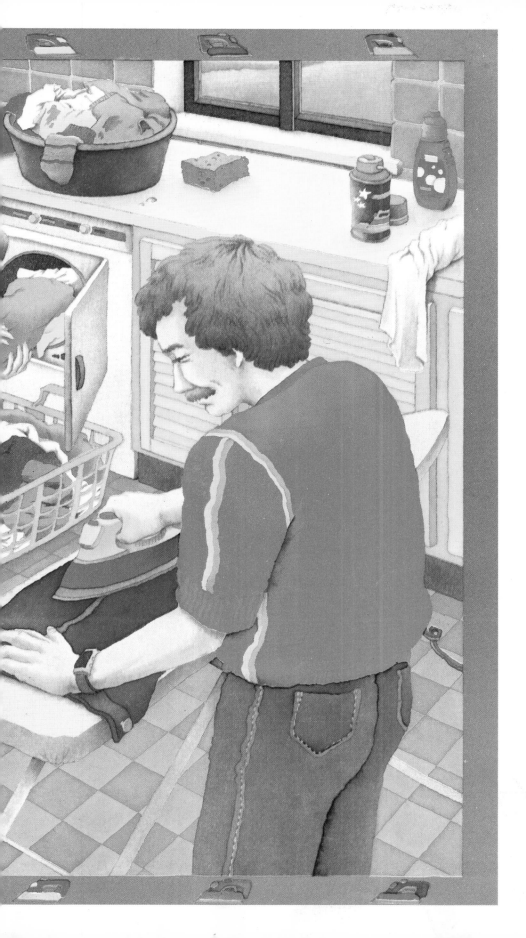

Working together is fun

Saturday is laundry day at our house.
We each have a different job to do.
Eric takes the clothes out of the dryer
when they are dry.
They smell and feel good while
they are still warm.
Eric gives the clothes to Dad.
Dad irons the clothes with a very hot iron.
Then Mom folds them neatly in a pile.
Peter helps too.
He is giving his toys a bath!

I usually help with the folding,
but today I forgot.
I was playing outside.
I try hard to keep my clothes clean,
but sometimes it's not easy.
I just fell into a puddle.
Mom teases me.
She says I'm so dirty, it would be
easier to put me into the washer
than to give me a bath!

In one week, we use a big pile of clean clothes.
Doing the laundry is a big job.
Working together makes doing the
laundry fun.

Picture talk

Which household tasks does your family share?
Why is it important to do laundry?
Which things in the picture help to keep
the clothes looking clean and neat?

Making breakfast for Mom and Dad

On Sunday mornings, Mom and Dad
like to sleep in.
We make breakfast for them and
for ourselves.

My brother Leonard is eighteen, and
my sister Carmine is sixteen.
They are old enough to cook.
Once I tried to cook eggs,
but they tasted like rubber.
Leonard cooks delicious sausages and eggs.

Celine puts the dishes on the table.
My brother Ellis and I put out
the knives, forks, and spoons.
Ellis likes to eat cereal for breakfast.
I'm waiting for Carmine's pancakes.
My little brother Nelson likes his breakfast too.
He gets it all over himself,
and sometimes all over me!

After we eat, we take breakfast
to Mom and Dad.
We like to do special things for our parents.
They work hard looking after us
during the rest of the week.

Picture talk
How do you help at mealtime?
Which breakfast foods do you enjoy eating?
If you could cook, what would you like
to cook for your parents?
What special things do you do for your parents?

We're having a family party

My grandparents are coming to visit.
We're getting ready for a big family party.
My aunts, uncles, and cousins will
all be coming.

Everyone is bringing different foods.
We're baking the desserts.
Aunt Jenny is frying some chicken.
Uncle Fred is making a delicious salad.
There will be plenty of good things to eat!

My family is special to me.
I live with my mother and father
and three sisters.
One of my sisters is a baby.
She is having a nap now.

I have other people in my family too.
My grandparents, my aunts and uncles,
and my cousins are all related to me.

There are only three people in my
friend Claudia's family.
She loves her family as much as I love mine.
Her family loves her.

No matter how big or small,
any family can be a happy one
if the people in it care for one another.

Picture talk
Who are the people in your family?
Which part of the dinner is this family preparing?
Which fruits are being used to make the desserts?
Which are your family's favorite desserts?

23

HELLO DAG HI BONJOUR HEJ

BUENOS DIAS こんにちは BUON GI

24

Grandma and Grandpa are here!

We've waited and waited.
Everything is ready.
Grandma and Grandpa have
finally arrived!

Diana and I run out to welcome them.
Grandma and Grandpa give us big, warm hugs.
They tell us they've missed us.
"My, how you've grown," my grandmother says.

My grandparents live in another city.
It takes five hours to drive here from there.
The drive makes Grandpa very tired.
My grandparents like their home,
but Grandma wishes they lived closer to us.
She likes to do things with us.
She says we make her feel young.

Soon my aunts, uncles, and cousins will be here.
We are all having dinner together.
My grandmother can't wait to see
her other grandchildren.
My grandfather can't wait to have a nap!

Picture talk

Do your grandparents live far away from you?
When does your family get together with your
uncles, aunts, cousins, and grandparents?

There are words in the border of this picture.
They mean " hello" in different languages.
Do your grandparents speak any of
these languages?
How do you say hello to your grandparents?
Do you call your grandparents
special names?

25

My family history

Can you see the funny car in the photo album?
My great-grandfather was one of the first people
in his town to own a car.
People called it a "horseless carriage" then.
Can you guess why?

When we visit my grandmother, she tells us
stories about when she was young.
Grandma liked to sew and play badminton.
I like to play with dolls, and I like
playing soccer. I can really kick a ball!
Grandma says I'm a lot like she was
when she was a little girl.
When I see her old pictures, it's like
looking at me in dress-up clothes.

Finding out about my family is fun.
It makes me feel as though I have
made new friends.
One day I will be a grandmother too.
I will tell my grandchildren stories about
my grandparents.
Maybe my grandchildren will tell their
children about me.
My family history will go on and on forever!

Picture talk
What family stories have you heard from
your parents or grandparents?
What are the names of your grandparents?
How was life different when the grandmother
in the picture was a child?
What would you tell your grandchildren
about the world today?

Working it out

Everyone has family problems from time to time. No family is perfect. The most important thing people in a family can do is talk about their problems with one another.

Here are five kinds of family problems. How would you advise these children to deal with these problems? Are any of these problems yours?

I am lonely

I am an only child. I wish I had a brother or sister. Sometimes I pretend my doll is my sister. I tell her all kinds of secrets, but my doll cannot tell me any of her secrets. If I had a brother or sister, we would be best friends. We would play together all the time. I would never be lonely.

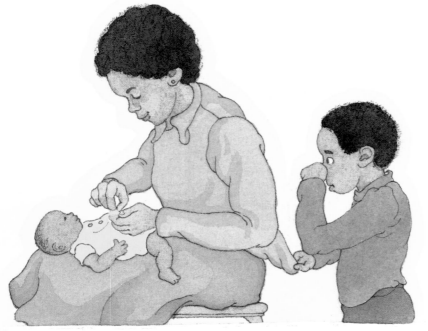

No time for me

I am no longer the only child in my family. We have a new baby. I don't like my new baby brother. He gets all the attention. He cries, and my parents both rush to take care of him. When I cry, they tell me I am acting like a baby and I should grow up. My parents never seem to have time for me anymore.

I can't win

Sometimes I fight with my brother. We both want to play with the same toy. He pushes me. He says he should get to play with the toy because he is older. If I tell my parents, he calls me a tattletale. If I hit him, he tells my parents.

She's going to be mad

Oh, no! I just ran my truck into a vase. Now the vase is broken. It was my aunt's favorite vase. Maybe I should pick up the pieces, put them in the garbage, and pretend that nothing happened. If I do this, maybe my aunt will not notice that the vase is missing. Maybe I should tell my aunt that I broke the vase. But if I tell her, she will be angry. I don't want her to be angry.

My dad yells at me

It seems that whenever I ask my father if I can go to my friend's house, he always yells at me. He yells, "No." I don't like it when Dad yells. It's not fair.

The Salad Family grew and grew

Ralphy Radish was all alone.
He had no one to call his own.

He asked Susie Spinach, who was in a bunch
To be his sister, 'cause he had a hunch.

He thought she might be lonely too,
And would welcome a family. Wouldn't you?

Then Susie Spinach asked Corn to be
The mother of this little family.

Mom Corn asked Mushroom to come along,
And together they sang this happy song.

"We are the Salad Family.
Come join us and live merrily."

The Salad Family grew and grew.
Now it has a Grandma and Grandpa too.

Twin Peas in a pod, and Baby Chickpea,
Bean Sprouts, Tomato; what else do you see?

Carrot and Broccoli too found a home,
And this is the end of our veggie poem!

Grandpa Cabbage   Grandma Lettuce   Brother Radish   Stepmother Bean Sprouts   Stepfather Tomato   Sister Spinach

Make your own Salad Family

Draw a large salad bowl.
Fill it with drawings of the vegetables in
the Salad Family bar.
Your salad should show the people in your family.

If you have a father, stepmother, grandmother,
brother, and baby living with you,
your salad will contain:
a mushroom, bean sprouts, lettuce, a radish,
a chickpea, another radish (if you are a brother),
or more spinach (if you are a sister).

If you have a stepsister, add broccoli to your salad.
Add a carrot if you have a stepbrother.

Introduce a Salad Family to your family

Now, doesn't all this talk of salads
make you want to crunch your
way through a nutritious salad feast tonight?

Why not ask your family to help you
create a really big salad.

Use all the ingredients you have drawn
in your salad bowl, but don't tell anyone
they are eating a family!

Salad sayings

What are the Salad Family members saying?
See if you can find all the vegetable words
the Salad Family is using in this conversation.
There are ten veggie words.

"There's not mushroom in this salad bowl."
"Don't squash yourself against me."
"I yam too crowded."
"The salad dressing always leeks on me."
"Mind you, it sure beets being in the
refrigerator. That's a place that
sprouts trouble."
"You're right. I think I've bean
complaining too much. I really
don't carrot all that we're crowded.
We shouldn't turnip our noses
at our home."
"I agree. Lettuce try to get along."

Try making up your own salad family conversations.

Stepbrother Carrot   Stepsister Broccoli   Twin Peas In A Pod   Mother Corn   Baby Chickpea   Father Mushroom

Your Story

Word helpers

These words will help you to write your own story
about your family.

doing words

share
argue
talk
cooperate
work
fight
care for
love
like

family occasion words

birthday
reunion
party
christening
celebration
birth
visit
wedding

family words

mother
father
uncle
aunt
brother
sister
baby
grandmother
grandfather
cousin
stepmother
stepfather
stepbrother
stepsister
twins
adopted

family jobs

washing
cleaning
tidying
cooking
sewing
fixing
repairing
painting
folding
vacuuming
dusting
taking out garbage
making beds
shopping

123456789 BP Printed in Canada 4321098765